THE QUEST
FOR THE ORIGIN OF
JOHN'S GOSPEL

THE QUEST
FOR THE ORIGIN OF
JOHN'S GOSPEL

A Source-Oriented Approach

THOMAS L. BRODIE

New York◆Oxford
OXFORD UNIVERSITY PRESS
1993

Oxford University Press

Oxford   New York   Toronto
Delhi   Bombay   Calcutta   Madras   Karachi
Kuala Lumpur   Singapore   Hong Kong   Tokyo
Nairobi   Dar es Salaam   Cape Town
Melbourne   Auckland

and associated companies in
Berlin   Ibadan

Copyright © 1993 by Thomas L. Brodie

Published by Oxford University Press, Inc.
198 Madison Avenue, New York, New York 10016-4314

Oxford is a registered trademark of Oxford University Press

Library of Congress Cataloging-in-Publication Data
Brodie, Thomas,
The quest for the origin of John's gospel :
a source-oriented approach / Thomas L. Brodie.
p. cm.   Includes bibliographical references and index.
ISBN 0-19-505801-1
ISBN 0-19-507588-9 (pbk.)
1. Bible. N.T. John—Criticism, interpretation, etc. I. Title.
BS2615.2.B76   1993   226.5′066—dc20   91-39137

3 5 7 9 8 6 4 2

Printed in the United States of America
on acid-free paper

To the students, colleagues and friends
at Aquinas Institute of Theology
St. Louis, 1984–1991

and to the Dominican communities
in Galway, Tallaght, Walberberg, and Biesfeld
for their generous hospitality

Preface

As Christians move into greater contact with other peoples the questions surrounding the role of history become more acute. First, there is the fundamental theological issue, still unresolved: To what extent are historical claims essential to Christianity? Few Christians would claim that the entire Bible is historical, but it is not clear to what extent Christian faith requires that some of it must be. There is also the strictly historical issue: What actually happened? If the theologians cannot resolve the problem in principle perhaps the biblical historians can resolve it in practice. But the biblical historians also have serious difficulties, and so neither theologians nor historians are able to move decisively. In a sense, and with good reason, each waits for the other.

The situation of biblical historians is not easy. The massive nineteenth-century quest for the historical Jesus has largely given way in the twentieth century to a quest for the historical church (for historical communities, and especially for a Johannine community). But, despite an apparently promising start, this quest has not been going well. Conclusions are fragile, if not contradictory, and the recent literary movement, like an overshadowing presence, has raised basic questions of methodology.

In the 1970s it seemed to the present writer that the discussion would be helped by making a brief attempt, as others had, to compare John and Mark, and in 1978 a half-developed fragment of that attempt was published in the annual *Seminar Papers* of the Society of Biblical Literature. But as time went on it became clear that the problem could not be dealt with quickly. It was proving impossible to conduct a surefooted comparison without knowing more about John's gospel in its own right and without viewing that gospel in the light of the literary movement. Was the gospel a rather poorly edited collection of traditions which were more or less historical, or was it closer to being a sophisticated literary and theological unity? Eventually, after the prolonged process of writing a commentary (Brodie, 1992), the evidence weighed heavily in the direction of unity—a conclusion which was traditional and which also tended, in practice, to lessen the emphasis on history.

In the end it has seemed better to separate this investigation from the commentary. The evidence here presented stands in its own right, and the commentary is rarely referred to. But if someone who is discussing the relationship of John to the other gospels and to history wants to presuppose that John is not a unity then the commentary should be taken into account.

The result, so it is hoped, is a study which will contribute towards clarifying some important aspects of Christian origins. It will not resolve the theological issue of how much history is necessary for Christianity, but on the historical issue of what actually happened, it should provide part of the answer.

St. Louis   T. L. B.
September 1991

Contents

THE QUEST
FOR THE ORIGIN OF
JOHN'S GOSPEL

General Introduction: The Uncertain Quest and the Need for a Firmer Foundation

> The origin of the Johannine writings is . . . the greatest enigma in
> the early history of Christianity
>
> Adolph Harnack, 1885 (*History of Dogma*, I, ch. II, § 3, suppl. 4)

The word "uncertain" does not mean that the search for Johannine history has not been valuable. On the contrary it has brought to attention a mass of interesting material. The synagogue ban, for instance, received fresh prominence from J. L. Martyn (esp. 1979, 24–62, 156–57). Yet, from the gnostic claims of Bultmann (e.g., 1955, 10–14) to the complex reconstructions of Brown (xxxiv–xxxix; 1979; 1982, 69–115), the entire search seems to lurch unpredictably from one fragile hypothesis to the next. And so, amid all the valuable insights, there is an unavoidable feeling that the enterprise needs to be more firmly grounded.

In order to clarify the full extent of the problem and of its progress to date it is first necessary to review it (Part I: The Uncertain Quest). Then, in the next major section, there is a partial investigation of the way in which a firmer foundation may be established—by tracing John's mode of composition, specifically his use of sources (Part II: Towards Establishing a Partial Guide to History: John's Composition [Use of Sources]). Finally a summary is given of the way in which the mode of composition effects the main aspects of the quest for history (Part III: The Quest Resumed: Initial Conclusions).

I

THE UNCERTAIN QUEST

The Move from Specifics to a Broad Three-Part Inquiry

Investigation into the history surrounding the fourth gospel has tended first of all to try to answer specific questions—Who? When? Where? It has proved difficult, however, to respond satisfactorily to these inquiries. The question of authorship—traditionally attributed to John, the beloved disciple—is extremely elusive, particularly because it fits into the biblical pattern of attributing biblical books to authoritative figures (Moses, David, Solomon) who did not in fact write them. It seems unlikely then, as with the authorship of the Psalms, that it will ever be possible to find out who wrote the fourth gospel. As for the when and where, one's reply depends on a mixture of argument and guesswork—probably 90–100 CE, perhaps somewhere between Palestine and Ephesus.

Partly because of the difficulty of dealing with these specific inquiries, it has usually seemed better to investigators to step back from the problem and to ask questions which, though more general (less focused on the identity of the author), seek to give the broad context for understanding the gospel's background.

There have been three main questions: What was the religious background? What was the purpose/life–situation? And finally, what was the history—if not of John or the author—then at least of the larger community (the Johannine community)? The three questions are interwoven and to some degree are increasingly focused—from broad background to surrounding circumstances and purpose to the idea of a specific community. However, despite their interwoveness they can be dealt with separately. First, the religious background.

1

The Quest for the
Religious Background

In seeking to explain the distinctiveness of John's religious thought, including his images and language, modern research has suggested three main influences—gnosticism (esp. Bultmann), Hellenism (esp. Dodd, 1953), and Judaism.

Gnosticism

"Gnosticism," a relatively modern word, is used concerning a wide variety of religious groups that flourished during the first centuries of Christianity. They generally saw the world and human bodies as evil, the products of an evil power, and, as a key to salvation from the oppressiveness of the material world, they offered *gnōsis*, "knowledge." "Such knowledge was diverse, although it generally dealt with the intimate relationship of the self to the transcendent source of all being, and this knowledge was often conveyed by a revealer figure" (Attridge, 1985, 349; cf. Bultmann, 9–10). The teachings of these groups sometimes contained oppressive structures of thought—for instance, concerning the evil nature of the material world—and partly for that reason they were regarded by many early church writers as false.

It is doubtful, however, whether gnosticism proper existed at the time the gospel was written. "There is no extant document which indubitably originated with the Gnostics from the first century AD" (Fujita, 1986, 189). This lack of documentation does not prove that gnosticism did not exist, but it makes discussion of the first-century situation hazardous. In claiming that the evangelist came from a gnostic background, Bultmann had to use documents from later centuries to reconstruct a hypothetical gnosticism of the first century. As part of that reconstructed picture he claimed, for instance, that the evangelist's sources included a collection of "revelatory discourses" (*Offenbarungsreden*) which was gnostic in its tendency (cf. Smith, 1984, 41).

Connecting authors with backgrounds is often hazardous, but it is doubly so when the background is hypothetical and reconstructed. Aspects of Bultmann's claim have been maintained by later researchers, especially by L. Schottroff (1970, 295), but even those who maintain it modify it. The tendency of more recent research has been to distinguish between fully-developed gnosticism (from the second century onwards) and various forms of pre-gnosticism (including Qumran and aspects of mysticism; cf. Fujita, 1986, 168–70). John apparently engaged these pre-gnostic developments, but he did not do so in a slavish way; his purpose rather was to steal their fire—to take what was best in them and, even by using their own language, to correct their occasional lack of balance (Kysar, 1985, 2415–16).

Hellenism and Hellenistic Judaism

There are several significant points of affinity between John and Hellenism (including Hellenistic Judaism)—points concerning the descending and ascending redeemer, pre-existence, witness, the "I am" sayings, the wine at Cana, and dualism (cf. Kysar's survey, 1985, 2421–22). The idea of the descent from heaven of the divine messenger is found even in such basic writers as Homer and Virgil (Greene, 1963, 26–103).

One of the key questions is whether John depended on Platonism, particularly Platonism mixed with Stoicism—the kind of Platonism reflected, for instance, in the documents known as the Hermetic literature (written in Egypt, mostly in the second and third centuries, CE; cf. Dodd, 1953, 10–55; Braun, 1955).

The details of the relationship between John and the Hermetic writings are quite obscure. There are several close affinities (cf. Dodd, 1953, 34–35; Braun, 1955, 259–99, esp. 259–65, 275–77), but they may be due to borrowing by someone who used John in revising the

Hermetic literature (cf. Braun, 1955, 32, 266, 277–78; Schnackenburg, 1:136–37).

What are more significant are the broader relationships. Platonism spoke of a world that is changeless and real, beyond the confines of space and time—and thus it is somewhat like John's idea of the real or true (e.g., 15:1: "I am the true vine"). Stoicism emphasized the *logos*: the *logos* was God, but there were elements of it in humans, and the ideal was that it should guide one's life.

The affinities are difficult to judge. Some basic conclusions may indeed be drawn: on the one hand, that John did not use the Hermetic writings (they are too late); and on the other, that the affinities with Hellenism are real. Thus the present state of research into John's relationship to Hellenism leaves one in a rather undecided balance.

What seems necessary to advance the discussion is some sense of the larger picture, some sense of John's general attitude to Hellenism as a whole. In other words, within the hermeneutical circle, which uses details to interpret the totality and the totality to interpret details, the point seems to have been reached when the accumulated details demand that attention be given to the broader issues. It will be necessary to return briefly to this question.

Judaism

In searching for John's background, the general tendency of recent decades has been to lessen the emphasis on gnosticism and Hellenism and to focus rather on Judaism. The Judaism in question, however, is not simple. Apart from being affected significantly both by Hellenism (Hengel, 1974, 104) and the roots of gnosticism (Fujita, 1986, 193–200), Judaism was in ferment. Qumran was just one symptom of a larger process of searching and rethinking. As Kysar (1985, 2425) concludes: "the Judaism we are seeking to unearth behind the gospel was rooted in the OT and related to the rabbinic movement, but also swayed by 'sectarian' features which might have included apocalyptic, mystical, and Qumranian characteristics." What this in fact suggests is that John has filtered and synthesized virtually the whole spectrum of contemporary Jewish writing and thought.

2

The Quest for the Purpose/Life-Situation

It is not immediately clear what circumstances led to the writing of the gospel. Modern scholarship has made five main suggestions.

A Conflict with a/the Synagogue

Nowhere does the emphasis on John's Judaic background find clearer expression than in this opinion. On the basis of the way the gospel refers to the Jews, and particularly the way chapter 9 speaks of expulsion from the synagogue, J. L. Martyn (1968, 1978, 1979) has proposed that the fourth gospel is colored by a conflict with members of a Jewish synagogue. Christians were being forced out, and the gospel reflects the atmosphere of dividedness. W. Meeks (1972) has taken this further by proposing that the gospel in fact reflects a group which is sectarian. Schnackenberg (1:165–67) adds yet another dimension to the picture of division: while granting that the gospel retains some element of trying to speak positively to the Jews, he regards the evangelist's basic attitude to the Jews as one of hostility.

A Mission to (Anti-Jewish) Samaria

This view takes its cue not so much from chapter 9 as from earlier Samaria-related texts, especially from John 4:1–42 (cf. esp. Buchanan,

1968; Freed, 1970). The gospel is seen as interested in Samaria and as reflecting Samaritan elements. As for John's anti-Jewishness, this is to be regarded, not as reflecting a recent conflict with or within a synagogue, but as springing from the much older and broader antagonism between Jews and Samaritans.

An Anti-Docetic Polemic

It appears to be implied by Irenaeus (*Against Heresies*, 3.11.1, 1, 26:1) that John wrote to counter the mistaken view that Christ was not fully human. To some degree such a motif is in fact present: from the Word becoming flesh (John 1:14) to the flow of blood and water (19:34–35), several texts emphasize the reality of Christ's humanity. Consequently a number of researchers, particularly G. Richter (1975), have seen this idea as important to John's purpose.

An Appeal to All Christians
(Jewish and Gentile)

According to this opinion the gospel was written not so much to counter some specific view or group as to appeal positively to Christians of all kinds. C. K. Barrett (1972, 1975), for instance, sees the complexity of John's views as constituting a multifaceted whole, something which, when taken as a unit, communicates a rich appealing truth. G. MacRae (1970) describes the evangelist as following the hellenistic practice of gathering a wide variety of elements into a unity. And Brown (lxxvii–lxxix) has underlined texts which seem to indicate that John's appeal was not to believing Jews alone; it was also to believing Gentiles.

The idea of an appeal to all Christians has found some support in the recent work of Takashi Onuki (1984). For Onuki the gospel refers to three levels—the life of Jesus, the recent life of the Johannine community, and the life of the community in the future (1984, esp. 165–66). Thus the community may indeed have experienced rejection by the world, especially by Jews (as suggested by Martyn), but the gospel, as well as seeking both to absorb this painful history and set it in a meaningful context, seeks also to move beyond it; the evangelist, in fact, particularly through chapters 15 to 17 and the commissioning of the disciples (20:19–23), shows that through the Spirit Jesus gives believers a renewable mandate to go forth into the world.

An Apologetic Against Sectarians/Adherents of John the Baptist

It has sometimes been suggested that, when the fourth evangelist was writing, there existed a group of Baptist sectarians—followers of John the Baptist who, instead of acknowledging the pre-eminence of Jesus, insisted on giving undue importance to their own master—and that one of the motivations for writing the gospel was to confront these sectarians, to provide an apologetic that would reveal their distortion of the truth (cf. esp. Baldensberger, 1898; Brown, 1:lxvii–lxx; 1979, 69–71). In order to illustrate the problems of reconstructing motivations, this hypothesis will be looked at closely.

The main problem with this theory concerns the reality of the sectarians—whether they ever even existed. Baldensberger argued from the prologue: the prologue makes an unfavorable contrast between John the Baptist and Jesus, and since the prologue is the key to the gospel, such an unfavorable contrast means that the gospel as a whole wants to put John the Baptist in his place—a purpose which is best explained by the idea that when the evangelist was writing, followers of the Baptist were making undue claims for their master and thus were causing a problem.

In the nature of the case, it is virtually impossible to prove the non-existence of such sectarians. All one can say is that nothing of the kind follows from the prologue. As a close analysis of 1:1–18 indicates, John is depicted as embodying the tradition of the ancient prophets—he is a positive witness, someone who cheers when Jesus finally enters. To speak of an unfavorable contrast between Jesus and John is like speaking of an unfavorable contrast between Mahatma Gandhi and his mother; it injects polemic where there is none. The difference between John and Jesus as found in the prologue—a difference which is real—is fully accounted for by bearing in mind the difference between prophecy and its fulfilment. No further theory is necessary, still less one that invents a whole social group.

What is true of the prologue is true also of those other texts which are sometimes mentioned as reflecting the existence of Baptist sectarians—texts which tell what the Baptist is not (not the light, not the Messiah, not the bridegroom, etc.: John 1:8,15,19–24,30; 3:28–30; 10:41), and texts which show his disciples asking anxious questions about the increasing appeal of Jesus (Matt 11:2–19; Luke 7:18–35; and esp. John 3:26–30). All of these passages, while telling what John is not, also tell positively what he is (he is not the light, but he is a witness; he is not the Messiah, but he is a voice like that of Isaiah; he is not the bridegroom, but he is the bridegroom's friend). They are further variations on the relationship between prophecy and its fulfillment. If there are anxious questions, including a suggestion of some tension, that is appropriate, for the transition from the old order to the new required a tense combination of continuity and breakthrough. The tension in question turns out in the last analysis to be a variation on the tension which is found in the Sermon on the Mount, when Jesus speaks of the relationship between the old and the new: "I did not come to destroy but to fulfil. . . . It was said to you. . . . But I say . . ." (Matt 5:17,21). It is a tension which is not foreign to the fourth gospel, for, as is seen, for instance, by examining the prologue and the meaning of 5:16–47, it involves a theological problem with which the evangelist wrestled, and which he brought to a resolution. Thus, in the prologue, the finished passage is shaped into a delicate unity which suggests that the tension can be encompassed within a larger vision. And such also is the implication of other texts, including those dealing with John; the tension fits within a larger unity. Never in the four gospels does the baptizer utter a word of resentment concerning Jesus; and once he has explained the continuity to his disciples, neither do they. The matter is resolved; the old and new, despite their differences, complement one another.

What is essential is that the tension, such as it is, is theological. It does not require that its elements be projected onto opposing sociological groups.

A further text to be considered is Acts 18:24–19:7. This tells of some people, particularly Apollos, who had received only the baptism of John. Completely missing, however, is any undue exaltation of the baptizer, still less any lack of enthusiasm for Jesus. On the contrary, Apollos reflects all that is best in John: he embodies the scriptures, and he teaches about Jesus (18:24–25, and again in 18:28). When these John-related people hear of the baptism of Jesus they accept, and there is no hint of resistance or delay. On the contrary: "hearing, they were baptized. . . ." And even as Paul laid his hands on them, the Holy Spirit came down (19:6). On the basis of an account which is so thoroughly positive it is not reasonable to build a hypothesis which is negative.

What emerges overall is that if one is to use the NT as a basis for speaking of the existence of unresponsive Baptist sectarians, one first has to project into the text an antagonism which is not there, and then take the further step of converting the antagonism into a late first-century social group.

In order to find a statement in which a disciple of John really does exalt his master over Jesus, one has to move to the third-century author Pseudo-Clement (one of several Pseudo-Clements). This writer describes a fictitious meeting held at Caesarea between Peter and Clement of Rome, in the course of which Peter tells how "one of John's disciples used to affirm that it was John who was the Christ, not Jesus" (*Recognitiones*, 1:60; cf. 1:54; see Rehm, 1965, 42). The statement indeed is clear, but as Brown remarks (1979, 70), "There are problems about this reference." One problem is that the original Greek has been lost, and the two ancient translations, Latin and Syriac, vary considerably, particularly in these passages involving John. Such a phenomenon suggests that what is being reflected in the John passages is not a fixed text, still less an ancient fixed tradition, but a theology which, even at the time of translation, is in motion and under development (cf. Brown, 1:lxviii). On such a foundation—the changing text of a late fictional story—it does not seem reasonable to say anything about first-century Baptist sectarians, still less to make the added leap of saying that such sectarians had anything to do with the motivation behind the fourth gospel.

The detailed study of Pseudo-Clement is complex and inconclusive (cf. Cullmann, 1930, viii). Rather than try to build on such shifting sands, it seems more reasonable to be guided by a text which is solid and pertinent, the fourth gospel itself. When that is examined, and when due account is taken of its theological dimension, the theory concerning John and late first-century Baptist sectarians appears to be without foundation.

3

The Quest for the History
of a Johannine Community

In recent decades a relatively new preoccupation has entered NT studies—the quest for the history of the Johannine community. Aspects of this quest were under investigation for some time—for instance, in the work of Oscar Cullmann. But it was not until 1975 that Cullmann's work was gathered into a single, synthesizing volume (1976), and it was only around that time also that several other researchers began to concentrate their efforts on this search.

The purpose in this brief review is not to analyze methods but simply to summarize results. This does not do justice to the depth and complexity of the various arguments, but it helps to highlight the extraordinary difficulty of the whole undertaking. (For sources, see Culpepper, 1975; Richter, 1975 [Eng. summary by Mattill, 1977]; Cullmann, 1976; Boismard and Lamouille, 1977; Martyn, 1978, 1979; Brown, 1979; Wengst, 1983. For some summaries, see Brown, 1979, 171–82; Kysar, 1985, 2432–35).

1975, A. Culpepper

The community was essentially a school, like one of the ancient Greco-Roman schools. There are a number of connections between these ancient schools and the Johannine literature, particularly that of revering a foundational central figure—such as the beloved disciple.

1975, G. Richter

The community consisted of Jewish believers whose evolving Christology caused them first to be expelled (from the synagogues of northern Palestine, Syria, and Transjordan) and then gradually to splinter into four communities (those who regarded Jesus as: (1) a prophet like Moses; (2) Son of God; (3) Son of God in a docetist way; (4) Son of God made flesh). Most of this process of evolution and splintering is reflected in the evolution of the gospel. First, when it contained the prophet-like-Moses Christology, it was a foundational, gospel-like writing, not dependent on the synoptics. Then, in light of the Son-of-God development, it was formed by the evangelist into the essential Johannine gospel. And finally, because of the docetist controversy, it went through a third stage: a redactor revised it—adding, for instance, the Word becoming flesh (1:14–18) and the flow of blood and water (19:34–35).

1976, O. Cullmann

The community consisted of people who from the beginning, even when some of them were listening to John the Baptist, were on the margin between Judaism and Hellenism. They were heterodox Jews and believers who were akin to the Hellenists of Acts 6 or even identical with them.

The central dynamism of this marginal group consisted essentially not of an evolving Christology (as in Richter's reconstruction), but of something quite different—a profound fidelity to the historical Jesus and to the beloved disciple's understanding of Jesus. Thus the distinctness of John's gospel from the synoptics is due in part to the fact that the historical Jesus had two different styles of teaching (Cullmann, 1976, 93–94). The Johannine community, as well as retaining the essence of one of these styles, retained also an independent historical tradition and its own strong sense of Jesus. Within the early church in Jerusalem the margin-based Johannine circle became distinct—it developed into a special Hellenist group. And through these Jerusalem Hellenists there was constituted (first in Jerusalem and later in Transjordan) the Johannine community.

1977, M.-E. Boismard

Boismard speaks not so much of the history of a community as of the changing ethos surrounding the various writers (three in number) who over a period of two generations (c. 50–110 CE) produced the gospel. At first the atmosphere was integrated and peaceful: around 50 C.E., some writer (perhaps the beloved disciple) composed a gospel which in many ways would have been acceptable to a Jew—the picture of Jesus was relatively simple (largely the prophet-like-Moses), and the attitude toward the Jews was not negative. Nothing marginalized here: it was written in Palestine, in Aramaic. But during subsequent decades (65–90 CE), as relations with the world and the Jews grew worse, a second writer (John the Presbyter, referred to by Papias) refashioned the gospel, first in Aramaic and then in Greek, and did so in such a way that the attitude both to the world and to the Jews was strongly negative. Furthermore, the picture of Jesus was rewritten—no longer simply like Moses, but far above him, even pre-existent. By now, for the writing of the Greek version, the author had moved from Palestine to Ephesus and had come to know a much wider world, Jewish and Gentile, and in particular had come to know the synoptic gospels and some of Paul's epistles. Later, at the beginning of the second century, the gospel was revised by an unknown member of the Johannine school at Ephesus.

1978, J. L. Martyn

Martyn's reconstruction is like a three-act drama. The comparison with a drama or stage-production seems appropriate because the action, as envisaged by Martyn, is unusually tense and narrow. There are no Gentiles in this play; they are not even referred to. Everyone who takes part, Jew or Christian, originally belonged to the same Jewish community, in fact to the same Jewish synagogue, and all the action takes place in the city or village in which that synagogue is located. None of the players is named or otherwise identified, and the beloved disciple does not appear. Nor is any clear name given for the city or village. What holds the drama together—and this is the essence of Martyn's reconstruction—is an acute sense of the developing tensions within this single synagogue.

At first (c. 40–85 CE) the atmosphere is harmonious: some within the synagogue have discovered that Jesus is the Messiah, and they tell other synagogue members about him, particularly by preaching. Their low-key message and manner are nonthreatening, and for decades all stay together within the synagogue, all as Jews and some as Christian Jews. During this time of peaceful preaching, one of the preachers gathers the sermons and traditions about Jesus into a form of gospel—something like a signs source or a Gospel of Signs.

But the harmony does not last. There comes a second stage in which the increasing numbers of the messianic group lead to a sharp reaction by the others—first by engaging in divisive midrashic debates, and then by two traumatizing actions: by formally cursing and expelling the heretics and by having some of them tried and executed. Those expelled react by rewriting their account of Jesus: no longer simply the Messiah, he is given a new elevated status, and, though he is from above, he also becomes the one who is rejected by his own (1:11).

Finally, there is a third stage in which those who have been expelled, but who still live in the same town, once again rethink their position in relation to their former companions. Their concern now is not so much with those who had never believed in Jesus as with those who had believed but who are now separated—some because they have hidden their belief and stayed within the synagogue (Crypto-Christians), others (the "other sheep," 10:16) because the persecution has caused them, along with other Jewish believers from other synagogues, to flee far from home. The final note is positive: the Johannine community (those who have been expelled but who remain together in the city) retain the hope that the good shepherd will gather together all those Jewish Christians who have been scattered from their synagogues.

1979, R. E. Brown

In comparison with the narrow drama depicted by Martyn, Brown's reconstruction depicts a community of immense complexity—complex in its composition and complex in its relationships. The first phase here is roughly the same time period as in Martyn (the decades preceding 85/90 CE), but the action is quite diverse: decades not of harmonious preaching within a small Jewish group, but the rapid coming together of former followers of the Baptist (including the beloved disciple), converts from Samaria, Jews of an anti-temple view, and finally Gentiles. Furthermore, it is within this initial period, following the admission of the Samaritans and anti-temple Jews, that a major event occurred: the elevation of Christology caused expulsion. (In Martyn's account, it was the reverse: expulsion caused the elevation of Christology.) Missing however from this period is the one major achievement of Martyn's first phase—the composition of some form of gospel.

The second period (c. 90 CE) saw the composition of the gospel (and also perhaps a move by the community from Palestine to the Diaspora to teach the Greeks). During this time the community is related not just to three groups (as in Martyn), but to six—"the Jews" and Crypto-Christians (both mentioned by Martyn, though with a narrower meaning), and four others: the evil world (which caused the community to feel that they were alienated strangers); the (unbelieving) adherents of John the Baptist; Jewish Christians (who, from the Johannine point of view, were not true believers); and Christians of apostolic churches (genuine believers but—from the viewpoint of the Johannine community—lacking full understanding). It is essentially through the pages of the gospel that Brown detects these six groups. Earlier, in accounting for the origin of the gospel itself, Brown (xxxiv–xxxix) had detected five stages.

Finally (c. 100 CE, just before the epistles were written), the Johannine community split in two. Eventually one group—the one to which 1 John was addressed—achieved unity with the Great Church; and the other, larger group, moved towards gnosticism. Thus the community's last shared experience is one of bitter division. It had often been thought traditionally that those around the beloved disciple were governed by his spirit of love and by his soaring serenity, symbolized in the eagle. And in some of the reconstructions already seen there are diverse pictures of a community that was tight-knit. In Brown's presentation, however, the governing image is that of two animals tearing at each other.

1981, K. Wengst

The scene proposed by Wengst is not of the very narrow kind suggested by Martyn, nor of the quasi-cosmopolitan kind indicated by Brown, but is more in the middle. At the end of his analysis of the gospel and of external conditions he puts forward the hypothesis that the gospel fits the situation of those Christian believers (mostly Jewish in origin) who lived in Gaulanitis, Batanea, and Trachonitis (in other words, in northern Transjordan—the southern part of the kingdom of Agrippa II). Within this region, according to Wengst, the situation was one in which political and military power was in the hands of orthodox Jews, and when some of those Jews became Christian they were subjected to hostility. The community was not a single group but rather a series of groups, small and scattered, insecure but still belonging to the Jewish synagogues. Then the pressure intensified—excommunication from the synagogue with all its social consequences and with accompanying theological confusion—and under this pressure the community faced collapse: people began to apostasize. In face of this movement—so many people leaving—the evangelist took up his pen and, through the gospel (c. 80–85 CE), appealed to them to stay, to "abide" in the faith.

As a way of summarizing these hypotheses, some of their salient features are now listed very briefly:

Culpepper: A school, centered on the beloved disciple.
Richter: Judeo-Christians, split in four, especially by docetism.
Cullmann: Jerusalem Hellenists, with a distinct historical fidelity to Jesus.
Boismard: A multi-document production, from Palestine to Ephesus.
Martyn: A synagogue drama (no role given to the beloved disciple).
Brown: A multiplicity of groups, of compositional stages, and of relationships; the community becomes two groups tearing at each other.
Wengst: Jewish Christians, in Gaulanitis, Batanea, and Trachonitis, suffering hostility, expulsion and apostasy.

Each of these reconstructions is built on a reading of the NT, particularly of the Johannine literature, and also of other external evidence. Consequently each has its own plausibility. Yet given the diversity of views, it is clear that the actual process of reconstructing is extremely hazardous. As indicated earlier, the gospel supplies no evidence, for instance, that unbelieving adherents of the John the Baptist even existed in 90 CE. The reasons given for their existence involve a bypassing of the theological nature of the text and in its place a projection of polemic.

Comments concerning these reconstructions have sometimes indicated their fragility. As Brown implies about Boismard, the process is out of control (1978, esp. 627). Negative assessments have also been made about of Brown's own work—that its first, pre-gospel stage is an ungraspable ghost (Wengst, 1983, 32); that its theory of gospel composition is unverifiable (Schnackenburg, 1977, 23–24); and that its final stage, concerning the division of the community into two factions, involves projecting into 1 John a polemic which is not there. In the words of Brevard Childs (1985, 483), "what purports to be an historical investigation is actually an exercise in creative imagination with very few historical controls."

Nor has the work of Wengst restored confidence. It has indeed received some support. In fact, G. Reim (1988, esp. 86) not only supports it, he makes it more precise. By invoking other criteria, and by implicitly leaving aside Wengst's image of scattered groups, Reim suggests that the community lived in one place. And with considerable exactitude he indicates where that place was—southern Gaulanitis, in other words, somewhere in the area touching the northeastern shore of the sea of Galilee, "not far from Bethsaida and Capernaum."

Reim does not discuss further possibilities.

But others see Wengst's theory as aggravating the situation—as dragging the quest in yet another unverifiable direction. M. Hengel (1989, 116) regards Wengst's hypothesis as "an invention of scholarly fancy." J. Kügler (1984) warns that Johannine research is being turned into science fiction. And J. L. Martyn (addressing the SBL at Anaheim, Calif., Nov. 19, 1989) has compared the stream of reconstructions, including his own, to a genie which has been let out of a bottle and which is "not proving easy to control."

The situation is not remedied by saying that one's reconstruction need not be exact, that one will be satisfied with a limited percentage of accuracy. Such qualifying statments reflect an appropriate caution, but they do not help the discussion; on the contrary, they distract it and confuse it. When one looks at these various reconstructions, these intriguing buildings, the question is not how many bricks in this or that wall are solid but whether there is any solidity to the foundation of the entire house.

What is needed is another approach to the problem.

II

TOWARDS ESTABLISHING
A PARTIAL GUIDE TO HISTORY:
JOHN'S COMPOSITION
(Use of Sources)

Composition as a Basis for History

Given some of the difficulties in tracing Johannine history, particularly the unpredictability of the histories which claim to reflect a Johannine community, it is clear that some guiding element is needed, some criterion which is more reliable.

The answer is supplied by Kysar (1985, 2435): "refinement of the history of the community will be made possible . . . as the work of the history of composition progresses." In other words, the historical quest is such that, in practice, the best available key is the history of composition.

To some degree this is fairly obvious and in fact is already assumed by many researchers. When J. Neyrey (1988, 15), for instance, reconstucts a history, he begins the process by speaking of apparent redactional levels.

Yet the priority of tracing the compositional process is not always given due regard. Martyn, for instance, jumps into the middle of the historical questions without pausing sufficiently to get his bearings from the larger process of composition (1978, 1979). In fact, at one stage he is quite candid about the matter: he indicates that time and space do not allow for a more thorough investigation of the redactional process (1978, 46–47).

Yet Kysar's principle is not to be circumvented: the primary path to history is through tracing the process of composition, and it needs to be done as fully as possible. It is partly for this reason that, before embarking on the present study, it has seemed necessary to spend so much time analyzing the text's structure and seeking to determine whether that structure forms a unity (Brodie, 1992). The fact that it does form a unity which is complex, precise, and sophisticated, suggests immediately that several historical hypotheses may be laid aside—all those hypotheses or parts of hypotheses which are built on the alleged disunity of the text or on redactional theories which depend on such disunity.

It is necessary, however, to investigate further—to try if possible to go behind the text and to discern some of its main sources and some of the ways in which these sources were used. If that can be done, if the underlying dynamics of composition can be uncovered, then the roots of the gospel will be clearer, and the search for history will have a stronger foundation and a better sense of direction.

This idea, of going behind the text, may suggest essentially the same process as reconstructing a history—thus raising the specter of simply adding to the list of unverifiable hypotheses. But there is a fundamental difference. The essence of the various hypotheses is that they seek to connect existing documents, especially the gospel, with a background which is lost. (Some information is indeed available about places like Jerusalem, Gaulanitis, and Ephesus. But no discussion of this information, no matter how learned or voluminous or careful, can hide the fact that the information is fragmentary and that the most essential elements are missing—including reliable information about the Johaninne community's location and even about its existence). Connecting the gospel with such an elusive background is like trying to build a bridge when only one of the supporting ends is solid. It is a process which is out of control.

In the bridge-building which is to be undertaken here the ends at least are reliable. Instead of going from the gospel to an unknown background or to an unknown editorial procedure, the present study examines the way in which the gospel is linked with other biblical documents, documents which, far from being lost, are fully available. This does not mean that the linking process will be easy; it requires both pedantic patience and sympathetic imagination. But since one can constantly check the documents—in a way that one can never check vanished societies—the process is more reliable; it is subject to control.

4

The Quest for Sources:
The Central Problem

It is generally agreed that the fourth gospel is based to a significant extent on some form of predecessor, an older document which contained a basic narrative concerning Jesus and which acted as a backbone or foundation for the present text. There is deep uncertainty however concerning the identity of that predecessor. Some would say that it was the gospel of Mark (cf. esp. Barrett, 42–54; 1974), others that it was the evangelist's own first edition (cf. esp. Brown, xxxv), and still others that it was some form of a document which put a special emphasis on Jesus' miracles or signs (the "signs source" or Gospel of Signs). Taken in isolation, Brown's idea of an earlier edition is quite possible, but it remains vague, and it is part of a larger theory which, as Schnackenburg implied (1977, 23–24), is difficult to verify. Furthermore, as one begins to appreciate the unity of the text, such claims about processes of redaction seem unnecessary and inappropriate.

The shape attributed to the signs source varies greatly. In particular there is not agreement as to whether it contained a passion narrative. Earlier researchers (e.g. Bultmann, Nicol, Schnackenburg), despite their considerable differences, generally contended that it did not (for references, see von Wahlde, 1989, 194–96; Becker, 112–13; Boismard's "Document C," 1977, 16–19, is exceptional). But, perhaps partly because of Boismard, two major, recent works, those of Fortna (1988) and von Wahlde (1989), maintain that it did in fact contain a passion account, and both imply that this earlier passion narrative was somewhat like what is now found in Mark—in other words an account which told of an arrest, a Jewish trial (of sorts), a trial before Pilate, crucifixion and burial, and, finally, a brief resurrection text (Fortna, 1988, 149–200; von Wahlde, 1989, 133–53).

There are two fundamental flaws in the various efforts to reconstruct a signs source: they do not use reliable criteria, and, above all, they do not sufficiently consider whether the predecessor was Mark.

The unreliability of the criteria is best seen not from examining the criteria themselves—close analysis suggests that they are based on a misreading of the text's difficulties, yet taken in isolation they often look eminently plausible—but from the diverse results of their application. Fortna and von Wahlde not only diverge from many earlier writers, they also diverge significantly from each other. In reconstructing the passion narrative both maintain the basic gospel story line (an almost inevitable procedure once one decides to include any form of passion account) but when it comes to filling in that outline—and the filling in is the real test of the method—the results seem unpredictable.

For instance, Fortna's reconstruction includes the accounts both of Peter's denials (John 18:15–18,25–27) and of Jesus' actual death and piercing (John 19:28–34,36–37; Fortna, 1988, 155–63, 177–87); but that of von Wahlde does not (1989, 134–48). Similarly, concerning the resurrection texts, the two reconstructions are markedly different:

Fortna (sixteen verses): John 20:1–3, 5, 7–12, 14, 16–20.
von Wahlde (five verses): John 20:1, 11, 14–16.

Obviously if Fortna and von Wahlde were present while the reader is considering these matters, they would explain that their respective positions were chosen with great care. Thus the nature of the problem is revealed: it lies not so much in the workmen as in the tools—in the unreliability of the various criteria. The criteria, in fact, are so difficult to identify and to handle that scholars could go on for decades producing divergent reconstructions of the hypothetical signs document. They could never quite prove any of these reconstructions, but then again no one could directly disprove any of them. And so the reconstructions would remain, each standing as a partial contradiction of the other, yet all united in the suggestion that behind the fourth gospel there was an earlier document, a predecessor.

Meanwhile there is Mark. It is not the type of document generally envisaged by those who first spoke of a signs source, but Fortna and von Wahlde have broken new ground insofar as their various reconstructions have moved closer toward something resembling Mark. And while

Mark may not speak explicitly of signs (except negatively, cf. 8:11–12), it does, in fact, contain them—in the many miracles of Jesus. Thus, in the search for the predecessor of the fourth gospel it seems necessary, before entering the hazy world of hypothetical signs sources, to check carefully whether the predecessor may be Mark. As D. Moody Smith (1984, 81) indicates, the search for a signs source does not become reasonable until it is first granted that John's miracle tradition is not based on the synoptics.

It is here that many of the proponents of a signs source fail most seriously. In varying degrees, the possibility that John may have depended on Mark and on the other gospels is either given short shrift or ignored. An example of this phenomenon may be found, for instance, in the efforts of Fortna and von Wahlde to find the text which underlies John's resurrection account. The problem is not simply that, as already seen, they produce divergent reconstructions. They also downplay the research of Franz Neirynck (1984a), research which indicates that when one seeks the text or texts behind John's resurrection account one begins, in fact, to envisage just such narratives as are found in the synoptics—so much so that the hypothesis of a lost source becomes unnecessary. In Neirynck's words (1984a, 179): "The Synoptic influence . . . may have been determinative for the whole composition of Jn 20:1–18." It is not that Fortna and von Wahlde counter Neirynck's arguments. They simply do not engage him; Fortna (1988, 195), mentions him but dismisses him. Thus, while they have made a certain breakthrough by implicitly moving the signs source hypothesis in the direction of something like Mark, they do not take the necessary extra step—that of testing thoroughly the possibility of John's direct dependence on Mark.

This reluctance has deep roots—at least as far back as 1938. Before that date the general supposition was that John, to some degree at least, did in fact know and use the synoptics (cf. Schnackenburg, 1, 26; Fortna, 1988, 216). Clement of Alexandria had reported that "last of all, John, perceiving that the external facts (*ta sōmatica*) had been made plain in the gospels . . . composed a spiritual gospel (*pneumatikon . . . evangelion*; Eusebius *History of the Church* 6. 14.7). And in later centuries the idea that John knew the synoptics took a more exact form: "In the era of criticism the theory gained ground that in all common material John was dependent on the Synoptic Gospels. Indeed even Johannine scenes that had no parallel in the Synoptic tradition were sometimes explained as an amalgamation of Synoptic details" (Brown, xliv).

In 1938 however, following form criticism's highlighting of the idea of oral tradition, a relatively new idea was introduced: P. Gardner-Smith (1938, x–xii, 88–92) contended that, in weighing the complex array of differences and similarities between John and the synoptics, the differences are so great that John could not have known the other gospels; as for the similarities, they can be accounted for by oral tradition. This approach was taken over and developed by several writers, especially by Dodd (1953, 447–53; 1963, 5–6), Brown (xxxv, xliv–xlvii), Lindars (25–28), and Schnackenburg (1:26–43, esp. 42).

According to this view, the essence of John's relationship to the synoptics may be summarized in one word—independence. And it is the idea of John's independence, an idea now well established at the center of NT studies, which makes it seem unlikely to researchers, including Fortna and von Wahlde, that John could have been dependent on Mark.

But independence is an ambiguous concept. A daughter who leaves a failing farm in southern France in order to enter the modeling business in New York may indeed become extremely independent of her aging parents, yet at another level she carries them within herself. There is a sense in which she is composed of them, and on close inspection she will almost certainly be seen to reflect them. Thus she is simultaneously dependent and independent.

Similarly with John. The fact that he is so thoroughly independent of Mark and the other synoptics does not, in fact, settle the issue of whether or not he is also dependent on them, of whether or not, like an independent offspring, he has absorbed them into himself and rendered them into a new form. What is needed therefore is close inspection.

In simplified terms the history of this process of close inspection may be said to involve at least three stages. The first was the process of careful comparison, which came to fruition in works such as those of C. K. Barrett. Even when the emphasis on John's independence was at its greatest, Barrett persisted in comparing John with the synoptics, especially with Mark. Though he did not succeed in unravelling the entire relationship, he indicated that between these documents there is some form of close affinity, an affinity which in his view was best accounted for through the idea of dependence (Barrett, 42–54; 1955, 14–16; and esp. 1974).

Secondly, there is the more recent work of what may loosely be called the Louvain School. Neirynck's study (1984a) of the close affinities between John 20:1–18 and the synoptics was not an isolated phenomenon. Since the 1970s, and particularly since 1975, he and other Louvain scholars have argued with increasing force that detailed comparison of the gospels indicates that John knew and used the synoptics (Selong, 1971; Neirynck, 1975, 1977, 1983, 1984a, 1984b; Sabbe, 1977; Van Belle, 1975). The result of their work is such that in 1987 Beasley-Murray concluded (xxxvi–xxxvii) that "the 'near demise' of the view that John was dependent upon the synoptics has been followed by a resurrection."

A third stage is the one which is given in the present study. The purpose here is to go beyond the examination of specific points of affinity and to provide, tentatively at least, an encompassing view—a view, for instance, of how John used the entirety of Mark's gospel. This purpose, however, needs elaboration.

5

The Thesis

The fourth evangelist was a wide-ranging writer, in some ways encyclopedic, who sought to produce a new theological synthesis, and who in doing so used a diverse range of sources—some non-canonical material, the OT, at least one epistle (Ephesians), and, above all, the synoptics, especially Mark.

The claim that John is an encyclopedic snythesis requires qualification. The fourth evangelist did not set out to integrate every detail and disputed question. Major events and central themes are never mentioned explicitly. The words "church" and "prayer," for instance, never occur. And there is no reference to the Sermon on the Mount or the transfiguration.

Yet it is a complete synthesis insofar as it probes the entire range of both the divine and the human—the divine plan in its full duration and depth, even from the beginning within God, and the human reality in its essential fullness from the years of facile optimism (1:1–2:22), to the time of struggling realism (2:23-chap. 6), to the final phase of seeking God even in the face of death (chaps. 7–21; see Brodie, 1992, chapter 4 of the introduction). Thus, it is a theology which is applied, a vision of God's Christ-centered providence which is written in such a way that, however high-flown at one level, at another is thoroughly down-to-earth, thoroughly related to the passage of human life. Here more than ever the Word becomes flesh.

And it seems to be encyclopedic also in its sources. Many events from the synoptics may indeed appear at first sight to be ignored, and the relationship to the OT and the epistles is even more difficult to trace. Yet, as will be seen, there is significant evidence that the evangelist did use these documents, and the fact that he did so is at least a partial indicator of a process of absorbing all available sources.

However, there is no question in this study of trying to prove the full extent of the evangelist's dependence on the OT, the epistles, and the synoptics. Such an undertaking would require decades. All that is given are soundings and overviews. A sounding—like an archaeological trench through a tell—examines one area in some detail and generally provides significant evidence concerning John's dependence on another text. An overview on the other hand, simply furnishes a sketch, sometimes very slender, of John's *apparent* dependence on a particular writing. Thus, in the case of John's use of the Pentateuch, for instance, one part of it—the dependence of John 4 on Exodus 1–4—is examined fairly closely, but the remainder is dealt with only in a tentative outline in an appendix. The distinction between the two concepts (soundings and overviews) is not always clear; at times the two overlap, particularly in dealing with Mark and Matthew.

No effort is made in this study to show John's dependence on non-canonical documents, yet what is said here has implications for such writings. An author who shows encyclopedic tendencies in developing a theology and in using canonical sources is unlikely to have ignored other sources—including those which were not specifically Jewish or Christian. This likelihood corroborates the view, held by Bultmann and others, that, however deep John's Jewish roots, he was in dialogue with the Hellenistic world, in other words, with the world at large.

John's Use of Canonical Texts: An Overview

As well as using Mark, the fourth evangelist also used Matthew. In simplified terms, Mark supplied the fundamental ingredients of John's *narrative framework*, and Matthew the fundamental ingredients of his *discourses*.

At times the fourth gospel's affinity with these sources is easy to see. In particular, John maintains visibly Mark's beginning, middle, and end (the initial preaching of John the baptizer, the central episodes in which Jesus multiplies loaves and walks on water, and the final events surrounding the passion). Thus the reader can have no doubt; one is dealing with the same Jesus.

But having thus secured essential continuity, John transforms his sources so as to produce a new kind of gospel. Mark's multiple episodes are synthesized into a few striking dramas. Matthew's discourses are thoroughly reshaped and relocated. The Sermon on the Mount (Matt 4:23–chap. 7), for instance, reappears elsewhere, particularly during Jesus' discourses in the temple (John 7–8). The whole procedure is rather startling, but to a significant degree it corresponds to the oldest testimony concerning the origin of the fourth gospel—Clement of Alexandria's report that John decided to move gospel composition into a new spiritual form.

In broad terms Mark and Matthew fulfil the roles which Bultmann attributed to his three main hypothetical sources—the signs source, the passion narrative, and the discourse source (cf. D. M. Smith, 1984, 40–42). Mark comprises the signs document and the passion narrative; and Matthew contains the discourses. Their content however is different from that envisaged by Bultmann. The signs, as found in Mark, are not at all in the developed form which Bultmann had suggested. And the discourses, instead of being revelations which are primarily and explicitly gnostic, consist of the revelations and exhortations of the first gospel.

Bultmann, in assessing the profound difference between John and the synoptics, implicitly pushed the development of that difference into the background: he presumed that before John started writing, some other person or persons had already reworked the tradition into a form quite distinct from the synoptics, particularly into the signs source and the discourse source. The proposal being made here implies that the development of the difference, the crucial turning point, did not take place in some irretrievable background. Rather it consisted essentially of the fourth evangelist reworking Mark and Matthew, and however profound the transformation which he thus wrought, we have the documents, and the process is discoverable.

John also used Luke-Acts—not all of it apparently, and generally not in quite the same foundational way in which he used Mark and Matthew, but in a way which nonetheless was important. Thus the Nicodemus episode (John 3:1–21), for example, is built to a significant degree on Luke's account of the episode involving the open-minded Gamaliel (Acts 5:17–42). In Acts the sometimes tense encounter is between the Christians and the Jewish authorities. In John the essence of that encounter has been distilled and transformed into the discussion between Jesus and Nicodemus.

Use has also been made of the OT, especially the Pentateuch. Here too, somewhat as in the case of Mark, John gives visible indications of essential continuity, continuity involving the beginning ("In the beginning, . . ." Gen 1:1 and John 1:1), the middle (the testing of the people and the giving of manna, cf. Exod 15:22–chap. 18 and John 6), and the end (the prolonged final discourse, Deut 1–30 and John 13–17). It is hardly a coincidence that the two books conclude similarly: by speaking of the uniqueness of the many things "which Moses did" (Deut 34:12) and "which Jesus did" (John 21:25). The overall continuity is not quite as clear as between John and Mark, but that is appropriate: Jesus needs to be more clearly connected with other portrayals of *himself* (as in Mark) than with the distant Moses. Yet the link with the Torah of the ancient prophet is strong and pervasive. Thus John's Jesus is ultimately Mark's Jesus, but he is also a new Moses.

Finally there is John's dependence on the epistle to the Ephesians, a dependence which is seen above all in Jesus' closing prayer (John 17). Both texts presuppose an overarching plan of God, and both are particularly concerned with knowledge (Eph 3:14–21, John 17:1–5), with Christ's ascent or ascentlike prayer (cf. Eph 4–6, John 17:6–19), and with unity (cf. Eph 1:1–3:13; John 17:20–26).

Further sources could be sought but it is better to concentrate on those already mentioned and to seek, at least in a general way, to uncover the process of composition. It is a complex process; one which, above all, involves the practice of literary transformation, and, before examining it, it is first necessary to show that such transformation was not an isolated phenomenon.

6

The Ancient Context: A World
of Literary Transformation

The literary study of the NT has generally been carried out in a vacuum. NT introductions cover almost every significant aspect of ancient background—religion, philosophy, politics, economics, social setting, transport, language, and so on—but not literature.

Modern literary critics apply a wide range of sophisticated and useful tools—but usually neglect the literary world of biblical times. There have indeed been important specialist studies: examinations, for instance, of the way in which some extra-biblical literary device is found also in the NT. And, particularly in recent years, there have been significant contributions—for instance by David Aune (1987, 1988) and Francis Martin (1988)—towards setting the gospels and epistles against the background of similar-looking documents of the first century.

But what is missing is a sense of the center, a sense of the way in which the greatest writers of the ancient world, Jewish and Greco-Roman, set about composing their works, particularly a sense of the way in which they employed bold procedures of transformation. One hears perhaps of the editing process which is implied in some presentations of Wellhausen's well-known documentary theory concerning the Pentateuch—but very little of the central dynamics through which many of the biblical texts were generated, interpreted, and rewritten. There are references to Greco-Roman philosophers and historians, some of them quite obscure, but not much about the compositional methods of such key cultural figures as Cicero, Virgil, and Seneca.

Given this vacuum, substitutes have rushed in to fill it. In place of authors there are redactors, in place of literary dependence there is oral tradition, and in place of the thorough reworking of existing texts there is the very limited reworking, which is implied by most gospel synopses. Not that redaction, oral tradition, and gospel synopses are to be dismissed without consideration. But they are extremely easy to abuse. Thus, gospel synopses are invaluable research tools, but in their present form they place such an emphasis on intergospel relationships which are obvious—often almost word for word—that they tend to standardize such relationships and to leave little room for the serious consideration of relationships which involve a thorough transformation. Likewise, the concepts of redaction and oral tradition may be valuable in certain contexts, but in themselves the two ideas are notoriously vague, and in biblical studies it is this very vagueness which has frequently been the secret of their apparent success: there is almost no gap in any compositional theory which cannot be filled by invoking undefined processes of redaction and oral tradition. As Caird (1976, 138) comments, "it is very easy to use a phrase like 'a period of oral transmission' without stopping to envisage what exactly it means."

This is particularly true in discussing the similarities between the synoptics and John. Gardner-Smith (1938, x–xi) claimed that these similarities can be accounted for by oral tradition—but he never defined how oral tradition actually works, how it could genuinely account for the relationship. The same is true of most of those who have followed him.

The confusion surrounding the role of oral tradition goes back especially to Hermann Gunkel (1901). It was he, more than anyone else, who adopted a model of communication which was based on societies which were nonliterate (the oral societies which were the focus of much nineteenth-century romanticism) and imposed it on a society which was supremely literate, Israel, the people of the book. His logic was unsound (see, for instance, S. M. Warner, 1979), but his influence has been pervasive. Both in OT and in NT studies, many commentators invoke or presuppose the dynamics of oral tradition, but rarely does a commentary pause either to justify this presupposition or to explain what it means.

Some scholars have tried to fill the gap, and it is appropriate to mention a few. Bultmann, working in Gunkel's shadow and presupposing that the synoptics are simple folk literature, saw the gospels as coming not so much from Jesus as from communities: "the literature . . . springs out [*entspringt*] of definite conditions and wants of life" (1963, 4). But despite all he said about communities, Bultmann never explained the central element—the actual process of producing the literature.

C. D. Dodd, aware of the need for greater clarity, downplayed both the quality and quantity of the role of the community. He downplayed the quality by maintaining that the role of the community was not to produce something new but simply to modify what already existed: "the materials . . . were already in existence, as an unarticulated wealth of recollections and reminiscences of the words and deeds of Jesus— mixed, it may be, with the reflections and interpretations of his followers" (1963, 171). And Dodd revised the quantity of the community's role by pointing out that the idea which had been imported from OT studies, that of tradition being handed on from generation to generation, simply could not apply; there was not enough time; the NT period was "less than a normal human lifetime" (1963, 6). Dodd, in fact, tried to bring some element of realism into the concept of oral tradition and, partly because of his efforts, the idea often appears more plausible.

Birger Gerhardsson, however, has realized that the basic dynamic underlying the making of the gospels remains elusive, and so, in a series of studies (1961, 1964, 1979), he has proposed a model which is radically different from that of Bultmann: Jesus used meticulous rabbinical methods of teaching and transmission, particularly those involving exact processes of memorization and writing. And it is these processes of memory and manuscript which underlie the gospels.

J. A. Fitzmyer praised Gerhardsson's original proposal—"a thesis which bids fair to open up new avenues of Gospel research" (1962, 442)—but also said that it could not, in fact, account adequately for the synoptics. It was too rigid to explain how these gospels came to be so different from one another. It is necessary therefore to make allowance both for "the well-known process in oral-tradition by which a nucleus story is eventually embellished and modified" and also for "the markedly theological formulation" which has been imposed, especially by the evangelists, on the sayings of Jesus (Fitzmyer, 1962, 445–46).

This advances the discussion insofar as it moves beyond placing all the emphasis on either the communities (Bultmann) or Jesus (Gerhardsson), and begins to focus instead on the role of the evangelists. But it leaves the central idea of the relevance of oral tradition unexamined. How does oral tradition actually embellish and modify? And do such embellishments and modifications accord with the data in the gospels?

In 1983 Werner H. Kelber—working especially on the basis of modern anthropological research—proposed that the whole concept of oral tradition be examined afresh. The result was a resounding emphasis on the idea that Jesus and those around him used methods which were oral rather than written: "As oral performer [Jesus] had neither need nor use for textual aids. . . . Jesus' earliest followers . . . display[ed] only tenuous connections with literate culture" (1983, 19, 21). But when it comes to explaining the idea, explaining what oral transmission means in practice, the process is not clear. Kelber suggests some governing principles—"social identification and preventitive censorship" (1983, 14)—but then goes on (1983, 31):

> Jesus' . . . words . . . were subject to the rules governing all oral commerce with social life. Some words will have come to an abrupt halt at one place only to be revived at another, while others may have gently coasted into oblivion never to be recollected again. The oral history . . . is a pulsating phenomenon, expanding and contracting, waxing and waning, progressing and regressing. Its general behaviour is not unlike that of the stockmarket. . . . Or to use a different metaphor, the oral synoptic traditions represent proliferating tracks going in various directions, some intersecting with one another, others bound for a head-on collision, some running together and apart again, some fading, some resurging.

Whether Kelber is right may be debatable (for reviews, see Boomershine, 1985; Brodie, 1984a; Dunn, 1986). But one thing is certain: the diversity of the various models—those of Bultmann, Dodd, Gerhardsson, and Kelber—shows that NT research does not have a reasonably reliable working hypothesis of how oral tradition actually functions. This fact alone does not discredit the very idea of oral tradition, but it means that the invoking of such tradition requires explanation and clarity.

Oral tradition can, in fact, do much. In particular it often enables those with good memories to recall something with considerable accuracy, sometimes word for word. And on the other hand, it may contain an element of uncertainty, which explains why orally transmitted material changes rather unpredictably. Thus, it can lie at the basis both of accuracy and of confusion.

But—and this is the heart of the matter—there are some patterns which oral tradition cannot explain, particularly those involving com-

plex coherence; unaided memory has its limits. Just as certain opera-
tions demand a computer, others demand some form of pen and paper.
As Ong (1977, 254) remarks in a related context, "Closer plotting
requires writing." Thus before using oral tradition to explain similarities
it is necessary to ask whether the similarities in question fall within the
limited range of what oral tradition (of any kind) can handle.

As subsequent chapters will indicate, the similarities between John
and the synoptics lie far outside the capacity of oral processes. It is the
literary explanation, and the literary explanation alone, which can account for the phenomena. It is necessary therefore to lay aside this
reliance on oral tradition and to look closely at some of the complex
processes which were happening in the world of literature.

An objection may arise. As well as similarities there are differences,
differences which are sometimes described as gratuitous, and it has been
claimed that whoever says John depends on the synoptics must be able
to explain all these differences. However, the matter is not so simple.
The fact that the differences are seen as gratuitous may indeed be based
on an accurate perception that John did not know the synoptics. But it
may also reflect a failure to understand—a failure (by the one who
claims gratuituous divergence) to understand either the extent of John's
process of transformation or the delicate interwoven unity of the final
text. In fact, until we have reached a much more complete understanding of the unity of John's own gospel it is not reasonable to assert that
differences are gratuitous. And at this point we are far from such a
degree of insight. The persistent invoking of unreal redactors, for instance, reflects a persistent failure of understanding. The most that can
be asked is that as our understanding of the gospels grows, so, piece by
piece, John's changing of the synoptic account should be increasingly
explained. In the meantime, therefore, the decisive question is whether
the similarities are significant (whether they exceed the capacity of oral
tradition) and whether, within the limits of our understanding, we can
begin to give an explanation of the differences.

Jewish Literature: A World of Rewriting, Transformation, and Synthesis

The literary tradition on which John ultimately rested, a tradition which
implicitly and explicitly he recalled over and over, was not something

narrow. From the opening pages of Genesis to the catastrophic fall of Jerusalem (2 Kings 25) and from the oracles of the prophets to the pithy sayings of Proverbs, the Hebrew scriptural tradition acted as a filter of world events and world literature. It encompassed everything from Mesopotamian creation stories to the practical admonitions of Egyptian wisdom. Nor did it cease to expand both in readership and sources. Already, centuries before John, it had been translated into the world's leading language, and particularly in its Greek form, had begun to engage Greco-Roman culture. Even at its most sectarian, as in Nahum and Esther, it could speak of distant capitals and of an empire which stretched from India (Esth 1:1). It was encyclopedic.

If John remained true to the spirit of that tradition it is unlikely that he let himself be isolated from the larger literary world, still less from those who had already written gospels.

But reliance on that tradition, including reliance on earlier gospels, did not necessarily mean that John would reproduce existing texts and passages word for word. The biblical tradition, however encyclopedic, was not static; it was not like a vast stack of assorted bricks in which each brick lies inert on the one underneath it. It was more like a living organism which keeps developing new forms and in which the new cells depend in some way on the old.

A good example of this type of development may be found in the book of Deuteronomy. As described by W. Moran (1969, 259, par. 225a):

> It is a *summa theologica*, an original synthesis, and in many respects a bold one, of Israel's sacred traditions, customs and institutions. The patriarchs and God's promise to them of progeny and land, the exodus, the revelation of Sinai-Horeb, the desert wanderings, the taking of Canaan, sacred festivals, ritual and worship, the law of sanctuary and city-gate, judge, priest, prophet, king, holy war, covenant—Dt brings them all together, stripping many to their barest essence, refracting others in the prism of its special concerns, but . . . imparting to all a profound unity in its vision of God and his people. It is a theology rooted in the present, a theology of reform, born in a crisis of faith. Though it is strongly traditional, it is not antiquarian; it reasserts the validity of ancient beliefs and practices, but it does not hesitate to adapt, change, even boldly innovate.

What is essential is that Deuteronomy is simultaneously traditional and new, dependent and independent. As surely as Genesis had filtered the old creation stories, Deuteronomy, in turn, filtered and interpreted the biblical material. And so the process continued—through the composition of the various biblical books and, in varying ways, through later centuries of interpretation—even through the works of the rabbis and the NT, including John.

The field, which thus begins to emerge, is vast and complex, often subtle. It is symptomatic of the difficulty of dealing with it that one of the most basic terms sometimes used in trying to describe it, "midrash," is itself unclear (Porton, 1979, esp. 112). Some use the term loosely to refer to almost any scriptural allusion, however veiled, but others argue strongly that "the central feature of a midrashic comment is its *explicit* relationship to the Bible" (Porton, 1985, 5–6). More substantive than this terminological difficulty is the fact that the entire field is largely unknown. In the 1950s, when Renée Bloch was setting out to investigate it, she described it as an area which was "almost completely unexplored" (1957, 1279).

Bloch was prevented by an early death from pursuing her goal, but several others have undertaken aspects of the task. Among these, two of the most significant explorers have been Geza Vermes (1961) and Michael Fishbane (1985; and much more briefly, 1986). Vermes concentrated not so much on the Hebrew Bible as on works which, though written after it, maintained its interpretive methods and which thus were "in direct continuity with the Bible itself" (1961, 127). Among these were a significant number of works which Vermes classified as "rewritten Bible"—texts which retold the Bible stories but which did so in new ways, particularly ways which defined and elaborated the biblical text. Thus *Genesis Apocryphon*, for instance, composed apparently between 50 BCE and 50 CE, and discovered at Qumran in cave 1, tells the story of the Egyptian sojourn of Abraham and Sarah, and does so in a manner which both takes account of the reader's possible moral concern about Sarah and also makes the whole story much more elaborate (1961, 98–99). Sarah is still Sarah, but greatly developed—more beautiful and more pure. And Abraham is correspondingly better.

Other writings from the turn of the era did much the same thing. D. J. Harrington (1986, 239), in his review of the phenomenon, lists the most important such writings as *Jubilees*, *Assumption* (or *Testament*) *of Moses*, the Qumran *Temple Scroll*, Pseudo-Philo's *Biblical Antiquities*, and Josephus's *Jewish Antiquities*. He claims that all "take as their literary framework the flow of the biblical text itself and apparently have as their major purpose the clarification and actualization of the biblical story."

Here too—as in the case of "midrash"—there is some uncertainty about terminology. Vermes's use of the term "rewritten Bible" had suggested that all these works formed a unified genre. But, however much they have in common, they are too diverse to be categorized so tidily (Harrington, 1986, 243, 247). Thus "rewritten Bible," while still a useful phrase, has to be understood loosely. It may be better, in fact, as Harrington (1986, 242) implies when discussing Pseudo-Philo's *Biblical Antiquities*, simply to refer to each document as "a free rewriting of [a] part . . . of Israel's sacred history."

It is this concept—the free rewriting of the sacred—which provides an important clue to the Jewish literary climate of the first century. The emphasis on freedom simultaneously gives a sense of direction and a sense of the unpredictable. One cannot say in advance what a particular writer will or will not do with sacred history; "each piece of literature has to be approached on its own terms" (Harrington, 1986, 243).

Fishbane's work (1985) delves more deeply. In effect, it traces later interpretive methods—in other words, methods which are often associated with later Jewish writers—right into the heart of the law and the prophets. Here indeed the text is not static; passages and ideas undergo varied forms of change. Like the inner world of the molecule or the outer universe perceived by Galileo, it moves.

The comparison to worlds in motion is not made lightly. Fishbane's weighty study covers four broad areas of "inner biblical" exegesis—scribal comments and corrections, legal exegesis, aggadic exegesis (virtually all exegesis which is not legal), mantological exegesis (concerning dreams and oracles)—and the terrain, which is thus explored, is dauntingly extensive and complex. It begins, in fact, to uncover a Bible which is "the repository of a vast store of hermeneutical techniques" (Fishbane, 1985, 14).

Some examples may be given. From the legal exegesis: ". . . two entirely distinct rules dealing with food . . . Exod 22:30 . . . and 23:19 . . . are combined as one rule in Deut 14:21. . . . The recombination of separate rules is also a transformation of them by the infusion of various . . . features . . ." (229). From the aggadic: the Deuteronomic law of divorce (Deut 24:1–4) "provided the substantive matrix for Jeremiah's speech [3:1, but] . . . Jeremiah has recast it twofold, in national and in spiritual terms" (308). And finally from the mantological: Daniel's ardent prayer from Jeremiah (Dan 9:4–20) combines an oracle from Jeremiah (Jer 25:9–12) with Leviticus's picture of the curses which descend on the sinful (Lev 26:27–45), and it does so in such a way that "the whole of Lev 26:27–45 has . . . been exegetically reworked through a *recontextualization* of its content, and cast as a prophecy of doom and hope for which Dan. 9 is the fulfillment and antidote" (489).

Rather than attempt to summarize this "vast store" of techniques, it seems better to highlight just two concepts—those of transformation and synthesis. "Transformation" is a word which, within Fishbane's work, runs literally from first page to last (1985, 1, 543) and which occurs in a number of headings (esp. 318, 383, 465, 500). It refers, for instance, to a way of changing the formulation of laws—"a veritable transformation of the meaning and intent of the original rule" (248–49)—also to the changing of genres from oracles into non-oracles, and vice versa (500–505); and especially to various changes of content. Thus in a single summary page (426) Fishbane describes how the content may be (a) spiritualized, (b) nationalized, or (c) nomicized (reshaped in light of the Torah) and ethicized.

"Synthesis" refers to various ways of combining texts: "Synthetic exegesis . . . operates on the basis of textual comparisons or associations of different sorts" (250). Further aspects of synthesis may be found in the examples cited earlier—in the combining of Exod 22:30 and 23:19 to produce Deut 14:21, and in the way Dan 9 combines elements of Jer 25 and Lev 26. And, along with distillation, synthesis was also seen to have been a central element in the composition of Deuteronomy.

The processes, which have been listed here—rewriting, transformation, and synthesis—do not at all exhaust the complex store of interpretive techniques which are found in the Jewish literary tradition. But they tell something of its diversity and vibrancy, and in so doing they provide a part of the background to the composition of John's gospel.

Greco-Roman Literature: A World of Competitive Imitation (Imitation and Emulation)

In contrast to much modern writing, with its emphasis on originality, ancient writing was based on the idea of imitation, in other words, on the reworking of existing sources, both of their form and of their content. Why this is so is not altogether clear, but it seems to have had something to do with the relative newness and rareness of writing—as though, amid a world still governed by oral patterns and still dependent on precious handwritten manuscripts, whatever had been captured in writing was something to be treasured, preserved, and thus imitated (Ong, 1971, 255–79).

The concept of imitation was not merely implied. Unlike the early Hebrew writers, who have left little literary theory, the Greco-Roman world articulated its literary ideas and, among these, imitation (Gk., *mimēsis*; Lat., *imitatio*) was central. Isocrates, a pioneering teacher of rhetoric, who was Aristotle's older contemporary, taught his pupils to imitate previous rhetoricians, and it was partly through his influence that the idea of imitation first came to be foundational to the process of learning to compose (e.g., cf. Isocrates *Against the Sophists* 17–18; Lesky, 1966, 582–92). The prestige of the idea of imitation was all the greater because it was used by Plato to describe all of nature (nature imitates a higher world: *Republic* 3.392D-394C, 6.500 C–E) and by Aristotle to describe all of art ("art imitates nature": *Physics* 2.2.194a 22—the sense used in Auerbach, 1953).

Imitation was not slavish. Closely associated with it, in fact often interchanged with it, was the concept of emulation (Gk., *zēlos*; Lat., *emulatio*; Isocrates *Panegyricus* 8.188; White, 1935, 11–12; Fiske, 1920, 40–50). Even while imitating existing texts, including texts which were old and revered, the writer sought to emulate, to do what had already been done, but to do it better.

Never in the ancient world did the process of imitation reach such intensity as in the two centuries preceding and following the turn of the era. The Greeks, of course, had imitated and rivaled each other, but the maturing of Roman culture brought a new dynamic—the desire to do everything the Greeks had done, and to do it better, to do it in a way which suited the new (Roman) world order. The result is that Roman literature is essentially a thorough reworking of Greek literature.

Among Roman writers perhaps the three greatest are Cicero (106–43 BCE, prose), Virgil (70–19 BCE, epic poetry) and Seneca (c. 3 BCE–65 CE, drama). These were not reclusive authors, to be discovered in later generations by esoteric literary circles. They were at the center of public life. Even the retiring Virgil was well known and was befriended by the emperor; his work was being taught in Roman schools even before his death (Greene, 1963, 72).

Yet for all their genius and fame they did not bypass earlier writers, whether Greek or Roman; on the contrary, they treasured imitation. "Let this be my first counsel," said Cicero, "that we show the student whom to copy" (*De Oratore* 11.31.90). He tended to emphasize the usefulness of having just one model (*De Oratore* 2.22.93) but on another occasion he expressed admiration for a painter who used five models to draw one figure (*De Inventione* 2.1–5). In his own work the practice of imitation and emulation involved a major process of synthesis: it was said of him that his writing combined the best characteristics of Demosthenes, Plato, and Isocrates (Quintilian *Inst. Orat.* 100.1.108).

Virgil tackled the most difficult task of all, that of surpassing and Romanizing the legendary founder-figure of Greek literature, Homer (see Conington, 1963; Lee, 1981; Knauer, 1979). In place of an extended war (*The Iliad*) followed by a long journey (*The Odyssey*), Virgil's single work, *The Aeneid*, spoke of a long journey which ended with a war. Homer's war had destroyed ancient Troy, but Virgil's war would found blossoming Rome. The relationship to the older work is an almost endless series of similarities and differences, some great, some small, some clear, others obscure (see esp. Knauer).

Nor was Homer Virgil's only source. Interwoven with the transformed ancient epic are several other writings, Greek and Roman. And the whole, though set in the distant past, is colored profoundly by the historical reality of Virgil's own world, its politics, its hopes, its human struggles. The result was quite extraordinary: during the beginnings of Christianity it was the world's number one writing. As C. M. Bowra (1945, 33) remarks, "More than any other book it dominated Roman education and literature."

As Virgil reshaped Greece's classic epic, Seneca reshaped its classic drama, particularly the fifth-century works of Sophocles and Euripides. His dependence on the older works is generally clear, yet, in another sense, he is quite independent. As C. N. D. Costa (1973, 8) says of his *Medea*:

> So far as we can judge, Seneca's chief model was Euripides' play, but he made substantial structural alterations, such as eliminating the Aegeus scene and reducing the Jason/Medea scenes, enlarging the nurse's role, and reversing the sympathies of the chorus. . . . Discussion of sources must not obscure the fact that Seneca's play is an original creation.

As in the case of ancient Jewish writers, there is no single study which provides a full formulation of the many strategies employed by Greco-

Roman writers in reworking earlier texts. However, some of the main procedures have been summarized elsewhere (Brodie, 1984, esp. 23–26), and they may be listed as follows:

Elaboration.
Compression or synthesis.
Fusion (a more complex form of compression/synthesis).
Substitution of images.
Positivization (turning what seemed negative into something positive).
Internalization (focusing more on what happens *within* people).
Form-change (e.g. using the form of a blessing to formulate a curse).

It may be objected that Cicero, Virgil, and Seneca had nothing to do with the NT and John. That may be true contentwise—even though, like John, the ultimate concern of Homer and Virgil was the journey and meaning of human life. And it may be true as regards sophistication of language—even though one could debate which are ultimately the more sophisticated, the polished lines of Virgil or the simple but penetrating images of the fourth Gospel. But as regards the method of composing—the craft of the word and of writing—the practice of these three writers is central; it was they who set the tone. In them it may be seen that the principle of imitation, which was so fundamental to rhetoric—and thus to the Greco-Roman system of education (cf. Kurz, 1980, esp. 192–94)—was not something to be discarded once one had learned a basic style. It was practiced apparently by everyone, from beginning students to literary masters.

Still, perhaps it did not touch the gospels. Could one not say that they form a distinct genre and are heavily Jewish. As far as is known it touched every genre, including history and biography (Higginbotham, 1969; Brodie, 1984, 26–32). Besides, many of the central genres were no longer clearly distinct. By the time of the writing of the gospels "the dramatic, rhetorical, and historical genres were well-blended" (Stock, 1982, 47).

Nor did being Jewish or concerned with Judaism mean that one did not employ Greco-Roman methods—as though Judaism was a world apart. Not even Palestinian Judaism was thus isolated: "From about the middle of the third century BC *all Judaism* must really be designated '*Hellenistic Judaism*'" (Hengel, 1974, 104). Even if aspects of Hengel's claim are disputed, there is no doubt but that there were several writers who, while dealing with a content which was primarily Jewish, employed Greco-Roman methods. The matter is illustrated both in obscure writers (cf. Holladay, 1983, 1989) and in Josephus (Attridge, 1976). And it is illustrated strongly in Luke (Plümacher, 1972; Kurz, 1980)—a fact which forms an indisputable link between the world of Greco-Roman writers and the world of the gospel writers.

Conclusion

One cannot say in advance whether the evangelists, including John, practiced the literary strategies of ancient writers, Jewish and Greco-Roman. If they showed no awareness of the Jewish scriptural writings, and if the NT showed little interest in the Greco-Roman world, then the hypothesis of literary isolation could perhaps be sustained.

But they were pervasively engaged with the scriptural writings. And however one reconstructs the details, the NT as a whole is a cry announcing salvation for the world. Thus the NT writers, including the evangelists, were thoroughly involved with both Jews and Greeks.

This involvement with the world, an involvement in writing, does not favour the view that the evangelists did not employ current methods of reworking texts. The following chapters suggest, in fact, that it is precisely these methods which help explain John's reworking of his sources, especially of the synoptics. These methods do not always explain his procedures as clearly and fully as one might like, but they do provide some essential clues.

This lack of clarity may appear frustrating. After all, in some ways it would be congenial and satisfying if one could identify one clear genre and one clear technique as providing the decisive background for John's procedure. But such a desire for simple clarity does not do justice to the nature of literature, to the fact that what is in question is an art, not an exact science. It is necessary to be ready to deal with complexity and subtlety. Ultimately there is no limit on the way sources may be changed by a particular author. In the words of George Steiner (1975, 424–25):

> We find innumerable formal possibilities and shadings of change. These . . . range from an interlinear translation of Homer to the Homeric contours in Joyce. . . . The [artist] . . . need not cite his

source-text. He can image, reflect, or enact it with greater or lesser fidelity. He can treat it in a limitless variety of perspectives ranging from 'photographic' mimesis to parody, satiric distortion or the faintest, most arcane of allusions. It is up to us to recognize and reconstruct the particular force of relation.

7

A Test Case: John 9
as a Dramatization of the Vision
Theme in Mark 8:11–9:8

Before attempting to give an overall view of how John used Mark it is useful first to look closely at just one section of John, the story of the man born blind (chap. 9). It is an appropriate test case, for as well as being colorful, it seems to reflect the heart of the gospel: it is physically at the gospel's center; and, as is suggested both by the work of Martyn (1979) and by further analysis, it appears to provide a window on what is going on in the gospel.

The appropriateness of examining the story of the man born blind is heightened by the fact that it is one of the pillars of the idea of a signs source—at least insofar as it turns up in every formulation of the theory. The amount of it, which is said to have existed in the signs source, varies from author to author (cf. Becker, 115; Schnackenburg, 1:66; Boismard, 1977, 17; von Wahlde, 1989, 190–96; Fortna, 1988, 109):

1941 Bultmann (28 verses)	9:1–3, 6–14, 16–21, 24–28, 34–38.
1965 Schnackenburg (3 verses)	9:1, 6–7.
1970 Fortna (6 verses)	9:1–3, 6–8.
1972 Nicol (4½ verses)	9:1–3a, 6–7.
1977 Boismard (2½ verses)	9:1a, 6–7.
1979 Becker (34 verses)	9:1–34.
1988 Fortna (4 verses)	9:1, 6–8.
1989 von Wahlde (24 verses)	9:1, 6–17, 24–34.

Rather than discuss directly the merits of these proposals it is better first to look more closely at Mark.

It is generally recognized that the healing of the man born blind has some similarities with various synoptic accounts of healing the blind, particularly with the healing of Bartimaeus at Jericho (Mark 10:46–52; cf. Luke 18:35–43; Matt 20:29–34) and, above all, with the two-stage incident at Bethsaida where, as in John 9, the healing was accomplished with the use of spittle (Mark 8:22–26; cf. Brown. 378).

The purpose of this chapter is to indicate that John 9 depends not only on the account of the Bethsaida healing (Mark 8:22–26) but also on the incidents which precede and follow that healing.

The Markan text may be said to consist of six episodes or scenes (so, for instance, Hurtado, 1983, 111–28; Mann, 1986, 328–54):

The Pharisees' signs-related hostility [contrasting background] (8:11–13).
The boat discussion about not understanding (14–21).
The two-stage healing of the blind man (22–26).
The recognizing of Jesus as the Christ (27–30).
Death and discipleship (8:31–9:1).
The transfiguration: recognizing Jesus as in some way divine (9:2–8).

The entire text (8:11–9:8) has considerable unity. Against the contrasting background which is provided by the scene with the Pharisees—their hostile request for signs shows a profound misunderstanding and misuse of revelation—Mark portrays a positive drama of advancing insight.

The drama begins with the scene in the boat (8:14–21), a scene which, because of its emphasis on the boat and the one enigmatic bread, evokes the reality of the church and of the presence within the church of the Christ and Lord. Thus it evokes the fact that beneath ordinary human existence there is an extra dimension of dignity and divinity. The disciples, however, cannot see it. Their perception of bread, and thus of life, is superficial. They do not truly hear and see; they do not understand.

But then comes the two-stage healing of the blind man (8:22–26), and after that there are two striking moments of insight. First, it is perceived that Jesus is not only a prophet but also the Christ (8:27–30). And then, following an emphatic statement that such dignity does not exclude suffering and death, neither for Jesus nor for his disciples

(8:31–9:1), there is the climactic transfiguration scene in which the disciples see that Jesus manifests a form of the divine (9:2–8).

In some ways Mark's drama is profound and powerful. In contrast to the hostile Pharisees with their talk about signs from heaven, the gospel shows that it is by looking at human existence and the human person that one comes to a true vision both of people and of God. It is no accident that the focus of the man's vision is on people: "I see people (*anthrōpous*) . . . like trees, I see [them] walking." What is being seen, however dimly, is the march of human life.

The Markan text (8:11–9:8) stands at the very center of Mark's gospel, and to some degree it may be clearly distinguished from the narratives which surround it: it follows the second miracle of the loaves (Mark 8:1–10), and it precedes the process of journeying, which will eventually lead from Galilee to Jerusalem (cf. Mark 9:9–11:1). Insofar as ancient authors frequently focussed a certain level of their works around their center (as around the middle of a chiasm; cf. Stock, 1982, 47–53), the central position of 8:11–9:8 suggests that within Mark's gospel it has a special place or significance.

Yet Mark's text is also fragmented and obscure. It takes considerable effort to put the pieces together and to begin to figure out their meaning. What John has done is to take this diverse text and transform it into a drama which has greater unity and clarity and which follows his own theological insight.

Mark 8:11–9:8 and John 9:
Introductory Analysis

As is shown in Table 7.1, each text consists of six episodes or scenes, and by and large John has kept the Markan order. Yet the outline is greatly simplified. When John takes over a Markan scene he does not use it in its entirety to form just a single scene of his own. He does indeed take its major element and use it as the major element of one of his own scenes—hence the correspondence which is reflected in the outline. But as well as the major element there are others, and these he *disperses* throughout the chapter, adapting them to his own narrative and emphases, and adapting the whole chapter to suit the larger requirements of the entire gospel.

The Pharisees, for instance, retain in John 9 essentially the same role

Table 7.1.

Mark 8:11–9:8	John 9
The Pharisees' signs-related hostility (8:11–13).	The healing (9:1–7).
In the boat, discussion and questions: understanding of the bread is either absent or superficial (8:14–21).	Discussion and questions: understanding of people is either absent or superficial (9:8–12).
The healing (8:22–26).	The Pharisees' signs-related hostility (9:13–17).
Jesus as the Christ (8:27–30). (The Christ-identity is secret.)	Jesus as the Christ (9:18–23). (For fear of the Jews, the Christ-identity is not spoken.)
The rejection of the Son of humanity indicates the cost of discipleship (8:31–9:1).	For the man, the cost of discipleship is rejection, including expulsion (9:24–34).
The transfiguration shows that Jesus is divine (9:2–8).	Jesus, revealed as Son of humanity, is worshiped (9:35–41).

that they have in Mark—their negative approach to the process of revelation provides a contrast for the positive progression. But instead of intervening just once, as in Mark, their role is interwoven with that of "the Jews"—a typically Johannine emphasis in the gospel as a whole—and they appear not in one scene only but on a number of occasions. First, in discussing the sign, they show the beginnings of hostility (9:13–17), and this may be called the major element of the corresponding Markan scene. Then, within other scenes, they are mentioned twice more, first as hostile and as involved in expulsion (9:18–23; cf. 9:24–34), and then as judged (9:40–41). To some degree at least, these pictures—of deep hostility and of alienation—reflect other elements of the initial Markan scene.

Similarly with the other Markan scenes. In diverse ways each scene is reflected not just in one Johannine scene but in a number of them, generally in about three.

Thus John's use of Mark 8:11–9:8 involves two fundamental procedures. On the one hand, he *keeps fairly closely to the backbone of Mark's outline*, to the order of the major elements. On the other, he engages in a process of *dispersal and synthesis*: while leaving the major elements in place he relocates the associated elements and blends them with other material so as to form a new synthesis.

However, sources and procedures alone do not account for the shape of John 9. The drama of the man born blind, however dependent on Mark 8:11–9:8 (and on other sources), is governed by John's own literary and theological purposes. Thus, even while using Mark, he makes profound changes. The notion of signs, for instance, which as reflected in the request of the Pharisees is negative (Mark 8:11), has been adapted to his own understanding of signs as positive (John 9:16).

The most basic change, however, is that the central focus of the drama has shifted from the life of Jesus to the life of a later disciple— one who, though pictured at one level as being with Jesus, at another is representative of many disciples in a later, difficult, situation. Through him the message of Mark 8:11–9:8 is given a form which is clearer and which is closer to the reality of daily life. In Mark, for instance, the cost of discipleship is a general principle: one is asked to take up one's cross (8:34–37). In John, however, it is a concrete challenge: the man has to face abuse and expulsion (9:24–34).

A further feature of John's adaptation is that, in unifying Mark's text, he also makes it much simpler. Mark's rapidly changing images have been absorbed into a single concentrated drama. This means that many colorful details are laid aside, but their essence is maintained, and the result is a text which for many readers is more engaging and challenging.

The following analysis is incomplete, particularly insofar as it does not try to trace John's use of all the details found in Mark 8:11–9:8. Should one, for instance, see Mark's geographical changes (the leaving of the Pharisees in order to depart to the other side, the move from Bethsaida to Caesarea Philippi, the bringing of disciples to a high mountain) as underlying some of the changes and developments in John? That Mark's geography has a symbolic dimension is widely admitted (see, for instance, Kelber, 1974, 62). In particular, should Jesus' bringing of the blind man out of the semitic-sounding village of Bethsaida and the subsequent going forth of Jesus and his disciples to the Greek-sounding villages of Caesarea Philippi (Mark 8:22–23,26–27), should all that be connected to the blind man's expulsion from the synagogue and to the subsequent finding of him by the Son of humanity (John 9:22,34–35)?

The analysis is also incomplete insofar as it does not take due account of sources other than Mark 8:11–9:8. Some use appears to have been made, for instance, of other healings—of the deaf man (Mark 7:31–37, note the emphasis on the idea of opening), of Bartimaeus (Mark 10:46–52), and also of Naaman (2 Kings 5; Brodie, 1981). The idea of expulsion from the synagogue, including the phrase "they threw him out" (9:34), is found in Luke 4:28–29 (cf. Acts 6:9–10, 7:58, 13:14,45). And the presence of the parents (John 9:18–23), for instance, would seem to suggest yet another source.

The analysis then will concentrate on the essentials. It traces the two foundational procedures—those of retaining something of the outline, while also dispersing and synthesizing other material. And it seeks to give some idea of John's guiding purpose and of the adaptations which he employed in order to fulfil that purpose.

Mark 8:11–9:8 and John 9: Aspects of a Detailed Analysis

1. The Pharisees' Signs-Related Hostility and Alienation (Mark 8:11–13; John 9:13–17, esp. 9:13–16; cf. 9:18–34, 9:40–41)

In Mark the Pharisees' attitude is hostile, and they request a sign from Jesus in order to test or tempt him, in other words, in order to show that he is not of God. Thus they have a false idea of revelation, and they use it not to build people up, but to bring them down.

In John, where signs are presented positively, the Pharisees are shown, not so much as having a false idea of revelation, as of misusing the true revelation: in the name of the sabbath they use the sign which Jesus has, in fact, worked as a reason for rejecting him, for saying that he is not from God (9:13–16). Thus John has kept the basic idea that the Pharisees use signs negatively, but he has adapted it to his own narrative—to his general understanding of signs as positive.

Mark's text suggests that between the Pharisees and Jesus there is not only hostility but also decisive alienation (Mark 8:12–13, Jesus sighs deeply, thus apparently suggesting that the Pharisees are a negative presence [cf. Brown, 426] and he leaves them). These obscure Markan elements appear to be reflected in clearer form in John's other references to the Pharisees/Jews as extremely hostile and as separated (9:18, 24, 34–35).

Apart from John 11:47 (and to some degree 7:32 and 12:19), these are the only instances in Mark and John where "the Pharisees" speak of signs. Thus, from a purely statistical point of view, the link between the texts is quite unusual.

2. The Tentative Beginnings of Recognition— Concerning the Bread (Mark 8:14–21) and Concerning the Man and Jesus (John 9:8–12): A Pattern of Discussion and then of Questions

The Markan boat scene refers to two conversations concerning the bread. The first is an obscure discussion (8:14–16), which in various ways suggests that the speakers are out of contact with the bread—they forget it, they apparently do not understand what leaven means, and they simply do not have any bread. Both in the text itself (with its enigmatic references to the one bread) and in the context (the eucharist-related miracles of the loaves), bread has a spiritual dimension, and so this multifaceted failure in dealing with the bread indicates a failure which is spiritual, in other words a failure of spiritual awareness or insight.

In the second conversation, however, when Jesus questions them (8:17–21), their slowness and blindness do indeed remain, yet, in contrast to their initial forgetfulness, they begin to remember. They recall, exactly, how many basketsful they had taken up. Thus, in the context of the spiritual meaning of the bread, they show the tentative beginnings of spiritual recognition. At least they have reached a certain preliminary level of awareness.

In John also, when the neighbours see the man, there are two conversations. The first (9:8–9) is a discussion which seeks to recognize the man, but which fails to do so (in the end he tells them). In the second conversation, however, when discussion gives way to more direct questions—the neighbours question the man himself (9:10–12)—there is the beginning of a process of recognition. With pedantic exactness—as in the case of remembering the number of baskets—the man recalls Jesus' name and actions. As with the baskets, this can scarcely be called spiritual recognition or insight, but at least it does show a necessary preliminary awareness.

Thus, in both texts there is a transition from initial forgetfulness (concerning the bread and the man) to later remembrance—at least of a superficial kind (concerning the baskets and concerning Jesus). In the context of biblical thought, memory and remembrance are not trivial topics; they suggest the whole world of recollectedness, awareness, insight. Hence, in both Mark and John there is a transition from an initial failure of recognition to a later phase in which there is at least some preliminary recognition.

John has made a fundamental transformation—he has moved the focus from the bread to people. Radical as this transformation is, it makes theological and hermeneutical sense. It makes theological sense insofar as it implies that the failure to deal adequately with the bread is ultimately a failure to deal adequately with people, to recognize their true identity—and such, for instance, is one of the implications of Paul's discussion of the abuse of the Lord's Supper (1 Cor 11:17–34): recognition of the bread has a personal aspect. And it makes hermeneutical sense because it renders a Markan gospel passage, which is unusually obscure, into a scene which, at one level at least, is easy to understand.

As always there is a further factor governing John's transformation—the need to shape the adapted text to the requirements of his own advancing drama.

The form which is found in the boat scene—the description or implication of a back-and-forth discussion, and then, with the involvement of other people, some questions and answers—is found not only in the scene of the neighbours (John 9:6–12), but also, in modified form, in two subsequent scenes: in the account of the Pharisees discussing the sign among themselves and then turning to question the man (9:13–17); and in the final scene, when the interchange between the man and Jesus gives way to a question between Jesus and the Pharisees (9:35–41). Thus at least as regards form, what occurs in Mark in just the boat scene is found in John 9 as a phenomenon which is more dispersed.

Yet this phenomenon—the discussion, followed by a number of questions—is quite unusual. Apparently it does not occur elsewhere in either Mark or John. Thus within these two gospels the link is unique.

3. The Healing (Mark 8:22–26, John 9:1–7; cf. 9:11, 15)

In place of Mark's two stages, John describes a process of coming to sight which involves six stages—beginning, in a sense, even from birth.

Yet the two texts are closely related. Mark's two stages not only implied the basic idea of advancing insight; through the enigmatic reference to seeing people as trees and as walking, the text also suggests obscurely that the advancing insight had something to do with the march of human life. What John has done—in a manner similar to what he did with the passage on the bread—is render the obscure implication into a form that is much easier to understand.

Here also—as in dealing with the preceding sections of Mark (concerning the Pharisees and the bread)—John disperses the source text: the account of the healing is narrated not just once but three times; it is told and retold and summarized (9:6–7, 11, 15).

Yet, despite the extent of these transformations, John's final text retains close affinities with that of Mark (see Table 7.2).

Many of the details of this similarity are debatable, yet the overall resemblance is significant. Some elements are particularly striking:

> *ptuō*, "to spit": apart from Mark 7:33, unique in the NT.
> *blepō*, "I see" (first person, present tense; Mark 8:24, John 9:15, 25): unique in the gospels and Acts.
> *epethēken . . . epi tous ophthalmous*, "he placed . . . on the eyes of . . ." (Mark 8:25, John 9:6, 15): unique in the NT.
> the picture of Jesus as sending one person and the use in that picture of *apostellō* (Mark 8:26, John 9:7): unique in the gospels.

4. The Recognizing of Jesus as Prophet and, in Secret, as the Christ (Mark 8:27–30, John 9:18–23; cf. 9:1–2a, 17)

In Caesarea Philippi there is a twofold process of questioning which leads to the acknowledgement of Jesus first as prophet, and then, following Peter's lead, as the Christ. In John also there is a twofold process of questioning—first of the blind man and then of his parents, and the result is essentially the same: Jesus is acknowledged by the man to be a prophet and then, through his parents' silence, to be the Christ. In Mark the secrecy which surrounds Jesus' identity as the Christ is quite obscure: Jesus orders silence but does not explain why. In John, however, the silence is given a form which, at one level at least, is easy to understand: the parents are afraid of being expelled from the synagogue.

Table 7.2

Mark 8:22–26	John 9:1–7,13,15
And they come . . .	And passing by . . . (9:1).
And they bring to him a blind man . . .	They lead to the Pharisees the formerly blind man (9:13).
. . . and having spit into his eyes and laid his hand on him	. . . he spat . . . and anointed his eyes (9:6).
he asked him "Do you see anything?" (8:23).	Again therefore the Pharisees asked him how he came to see.
And looking up he replied I see people . . . (8:24).	But he said to them,
So again he placed his hands on his eyes and he looked and was restored and saw everything clearly (8:25).	"He placed clay on my eyes and I washed and I see" (9:15).
And he sent him . . . saying "Do not enter . . ." (8:26).	And he told him, "Go wash in . . . Siloam," interpreted sent (9:7).

The introduction of the parents represents quite an elaboration, one which is very different from the elaboration found in Matthew—the solemn commissioning of Peter (Matt 16:16–20). In fact, the two elaborations suggest a diversity of emphasis: Matthew's text moves responsibility for understanding the Christ towards the authority of Peter; but John moves it from the parents back to the maturing person.

Here, as in reworking the preceding Markan passages, John has adapted the text into a form where the elements are more dispersed. The initial picture of Jesus and his disciples going on their way and of his questioning them (Mark 8:27a) would seem to have contributed to John's initial picture of Jesus passing by and being questioned by his disciples (9:1–2a). More obvious is the dispersing of the references to Jesus as prophet and Christ. In Mark "prophet(s)" and "Christ" occur within one scene, in successive verses (8:28–29); in John they are at the end of successive scenes (9:17, 22).

The questioning accounts (Mark 8:27, 29–30; John 9:17, 19, 21) contain significant similarities. While other texts do indeed indicate that Jesus is prophet and Christ (John 4:19, 25–26, 7:40–41), there are no other passages, either in Mark or John, where this twofold revelation (explicit or implied) is brought about by a twofold process of questioning people. Thus, within Mark and John, the link is unique.

5. The Context and Cost of Discipleship: Jesus' Impending Death, Rejection by the World, and Judgment (Mark 8:31–9:1, John 9:4, 24–31, 39–41)

The fact that Jesus is the Christ or anointed, and the accompanying implication that he has a profound dignity, that he is very special, could lead to the idea that for him, and ultimately for all people, life should be easy. Surely being special means being pampered. Such, in fact, is the attitude of Peter: he grasps the dignity but misunderstands its implications.

To avert any such misunderstanding Mark's gospel goes on to give a sobering summary of life—life as governed by mortality, by the need for detachment, and by judgment. The mortality is shown by the fact that Jesus will be rejected and killed; he is the dignified Christ, but he is also the suffering Son of humanity (8:31–33). The need for detached discipleship—this is the centerpiece of the text—is found in the picture of denying oneself, of taking one's cross, and letting go of the world (8:34–37). And finally, in the reference to the power-filled coming of the Son of humanity, there is a reminder of impending judgment (8:38–9:1).

In John 9 the reference to Jesus as the Christ is followed by the scene in which, under pressure from the authorities' hostile questions, the blind man emerges as a tough-minded disciple of Jesus, able to resist pressure and to endure insults and threats. Thus the centerpiece of the Markan text—the general principle of detached discipleship (8:34–37)—is found in John in a form that is practical, down-to-earth.

However, despite this basic correspondence, a closer examination of the texts suggests that, as with the preceding passages, the Markan material (8:31–9:1) is reproduced in John 9 in a form that is dispersed. Thus the initial emphasis on mortality—the Son of humanity *must* die (*dei*—providential necessity, 8:31–33)—is found in varied form almost at the beginning of John 9: it is necessary (*dei*) to work, for night (death) is coming (9:4). Thus both texts evoke aspects of providential necessity, Mark the final (future) aspect, John the aspect which is present. And the concluding emphasis on impending judgment, on the coming of the Son of humanity (8:38–9:1), is reflected at the very end of John 9 when, following the revelation of Jesus as the Son of humanity, he speaks of judgment and, in the case of the Pharisees, renders it (9:39–41).

John's reworking is consistent. In the picture of mortality (9:4), the emphasis falls not so much on the ultimate fact of death as on its implications for the present—the need to work, to get on with life. In portraying a disciple (9:24–34), the emphasis is not so much on general principles as on what discipleship means in practice. And judgment (9:39–41), instead of being in the distance with the holy angels, is here and now.

There are significant affinities of detail. Both texts contain some form of a contrast between "God" and sinful "humans" (*anthrōpos*): Peter, being Satanlike, thinks the thoughts not of God but of humans (Mark 8:33); and in John 9, it emerges that Jesus is not a sinful human (*anthrōpos hamartōlos*), but is of God (9:24, 31–33). Though the words "God" and "human" are obviously very common in the NT, such a contrast is not; it occurs only three other times in Mark (7:8, 10:9 and 27) and two other times in John (10:33, 12:43).

The precise idea of willing or wishing (*thelō*) to become a disciple or follower is found in both texts (Mark 8:34–35, John 9:27), but—apart from the reuse of Mark's phrase in Matthew and Luke—does not occur elsewhere in the NT. The similarity is strengthened by a further detail, one which is found nowhere else in Mark or John: *thelō* occurs within the context of a double, parallel, usage of the word:

Mark 8:34,35:   "If anyone wills. . . . For whoever wills. . . ."
John 9:27   " . . . do you will? . . . Do you also will? . . ."

Thus John has kept the word *thelō* but has made a typical adaptation: it is used not to express general principles ("anyone/whoever") but to pose a question concerning a practical down-to-earth decision ("Do you will?").

6. The Light-Giving Revelation of the Son of Humanity (Mark 9:2–8, the Transfiguration; John 9:35–41; cf. 9:5, 28b–30)

Having established what might be called some of the humbler aspects of human existence, Mark goes on, in the transfiguration scene, to indicate a dimension which is dramatically different, even divine. First, set in a different time and place (after six days, on a high mountain), there is an extraordinary physical phenomenon—the unearthly brightness (9:2–3). Then, in a development which crosses the barriers even of death, there is communication with Elijah and Moses (9:4–6). And finally there is the ultimate barrier-breaking communication—the voice of the divine, declaring love and asking for hearing (9:7–8).

In John also the final scene (9:35–41, esp. 9:35–38) consists of a climactic communication. The man who shortly before had been facing pressure and abuse is now encountered by Jesus and, following the revelation that Jesus is the Son of humanity, the man declares his faith and worships. In other words, instead of an extraordinary external drama—the high mountain and the voice from the cloud—John portrays a scene which, while involving a genuine communication with the divine, fits into the rhythm of the man's human life and development. Thus in both texts Jesus is revealed as divine, but the Johannine picture is much more down-to-earth. And while the Markan text simply implies the need to believe in Jesus ("hear him"), the Johannine scene shows the man as actually responding to that appeal ("I believe, Lord . . .").

Again, as with preceding texts, John appears to use the Markan text in a way that is dispersed. The initial picture of Jesus' unearthly brightness (Mark 8:2–3) would seem, given the context, to have provided material for the statement that Jesus is the light of the world (9:5), but this material has, of course, been conformed to the general lines of John's larger narrative, particularly to the earlier description of Jesus as the light of the world (8:12). And the further picture, of communication with Elijah and Moses (Mark 8:4–6), appears to have contributed to the depiction of the Jews as insisting on the need to be in the tradition of Moses (9:28b–30).

But again John is consistently more down-to-earth. The light, instead of being on an exotic mountain, is in human life ("while I am in the world"), especially in the light of faith as found increasingly in the healed man. The need to respect Moses and yet to go beyond him to the new event in Jesus—such is the implication in both texts—means not that one has to have an ethereal vision of both, but that one comes to this realization through human processes of seeking courageously and honestly (Mark 9:4–6, John 9:28b–30).

There are linguistic connections, particularly concerning Moses:

Mark 9:4–6:   Moses . . . speaking (*syn-laleō*) with Jesus.
                ". . . and one for Moses . . ."
                "For he did not know what to answer."
John 9:28b–30: "We are disciples of Moses."
                "We know God spoke (*laleō*) to Moses."
                "He answered ". . . you do not know."

Successive references to Moses, as found in each of these texts, are relatively rare (only a total of three other instances in Mark and John— Mark 10:3–4; John 5:45–46, 7:22–23). Rarer still are references to Moses in any kind of divine or heavenly conversation. Usually in the NT he is simply the source of the Law. In fact, apart from the transfiguration scene as taken over by Matthew and Luke, these two texts (Mark 9:4, John 9:29) are the only gospel passages which speak of Moses as involved in such a conversation, and they are the only references in the NT which use a form of *laleō* to describe that conversation.

Summary of the Adaptations

Having analyzed the text in some detail, it is now possible to move beyond the two procedures which were highlighted earlier (keeping the general outline and dispersing), and to look more closely at the substance of John's adaptations.

Overall, his treatment of Mark 8:11–9:8 shows the following persistent aims: clarification, synthesis, down-to-earth application, and focusing on the present.

Clarification is seen in the replacement of Markan images, which are obscure or apparently insignificant, by images or words which, even if they are sometimes more abstract or theological, are nonetheless simpler, more explicit and intelligible. For instance, in place of glistening clothes, John speaks of light, and in place of enigmatic suggestions of tension with a Jewish group (the Pharisees), he tells of expulsion by the Jews.

Synthesis has several aspects. The multiplicity of *episodes* and the enigmatic relationship between them gives way to a single complex episode in which all the parts are clearly interwoven. The multiplicity of *places* gives way to a single complex place. The multiplicity of *charac-*

ters (Pharisees, "this generation," Herod, a blind man, the disciples, Peter, the three disciples) is reduced for all practical purposes to a simple stark contrast: on the one hand, a simple open-minded disciple; on the other, the Pharisees and "the Jews." The opinion that Jesus might be any one of a number of prophetic figures is replaced by the opinion that Jesus is quite simply "a prophet." And the image of both Elijah and Moses gives way to the single central image of Moses. The multiplicity and variety of *images and words* gives way, in large part, to variations on the basic pervasive vocabulary of seeing and not seeing, vision and blindness.

Down-to-earth application refers to John's practice of developing and concretizing what is often merely suggested in Mark. In place of Mark's general principle that the Messiahship of Jesus is not to be spoken of, John tells of an actual couple who do not want to speak of it. While Mark speaks of Jesus' acceptance of Jewish rejection and of the general principle of accepting the cross, John describes real-life situations in which people are faced with Jewish rejection and ridicule. While Mark suggests that the transfiguration of Jesus has something to do with the disciples—he was transformed "before them"—John shows Jesus as actually transforming in a down-to-earth way a man who is to be a disciple. While the climactic manifestation of Jesus in Mark calls on the disciples to hear him, the climactic manifestation in John shows the disciple not only as hearing, but as actually responding in faith. And it is probably in light of this same process of application that one should view the relationship of Mark 8:14–21 to John 9:8–12: while Mark speaks enigmatically of the difficulty of recognizing the bread, John speaks concretely of people trying to recognize the body—the body or person of Jesus and his disciple.

Focusing on the present is seen in the lessening of Mark's emphasis on the future. Thus the future coming of the Son of humanity and of the power of God (Mark 8:38–9:1) is replaced by images of a Jesus who is already exercising judgment and already manifesting God's power (John 9:39, 33).

Associated with John's emphasis on the present is his emphasis on the past, i.e., on the time leading up to the present. In other words, while Mark emphasizes the time-span between the present and future, John emphasizes the time-span between the past and the present. In both cases the focal point—future (Mark) or present (John)—is not an isolated moment, rather it is the culmination of the preceding period.

Hence, not only does John tend to bring Mark's references to the future back into the present, but he tends also to push some of Mark's present elements back into the past. Thus the blind man becomes the man who had been *born* blind; the reference to Moses in the present (Mark 9:4–5) becomes a reference to Moses in the past (John 9:28b–29); and the cure is set in the context of all of past time up to the present (John 9:32: "Since the world began it was never heard that anyone opened . . ."). Hence the general rule that "John shifts the focus from the future to the present" (Schnackenburg, 2:426) is not just a detached theological principle. It is a principle which is expressed in literary details, in the refocusing of specific Markan episodes and phrases.

These principles—clarification, synthesizing, down-to-earth application, and focusing on the present—are fairly clear and reasonable, but the simultaneous application of all four may change very greatly the text to which they are applied, and such is the case with Mark 8:11–9:8. It has been transformed.

Assessing the Evidence

One of the pitfalls in assessing the relationship between two texts is to dwell unduly on the differences. Thus on the question of whether the shepherd theme in John 10 is dependent on the similar theme in Ezekiel 34, Bultmann (367) points to the dissimilarities and decides against major dependence. Yet as Brown (397) points out, the dissimilarities, however great, do not clinch the issue. The question rather is "whether there is sufficient similarity to suggest that the OT supplied the raw material for . . . [a] creative reinterpretation."

A further hazard is to dwell unduly on evidence which is weak. Insistence on evidence which is weak, whether by the one presenting the case or by someone opposing it, tends to distract from the central question: is there evidence which is strong, evidence which goes well beyond the range of coincidence?

In the question of whether John 9 used Mark 8:11–9:8, the evidence seems to be strong, and even the differences are generally understandable. There are three main factors: extrinsic plausibility, intrinsic similarity of the texts, and the consistency and reasonableness of the differences.

Extrinsic Plausibility

John's transforming of Mark's text fits broadly into the background of the many transformative practices which are found among both Jewish and Greco-Roman writers. The process highlighted by Vermes (1961, 127, 98–99), for instance, of elaborately rewriting sacred history, provides a partial precedent for John's complex reworking of Mark. He has taken a single incident, Mark's healing of the blind man, and with the help of other material, particularly from the rest of Mark 8:11–9:8, has rewritten it elaborately. To a certain extent Brown (xxxv) had envisaged some such process: he spoke of a stage in which "some of the stories of Jesus' miracles . . . were developed into superb dramas, for example, ch. ix." And to a certain extent some such process was also envisaged by those who spoke of a signs source. Fortna (1970, 70–74; 1988, 109), for instance, suggested at different times that the original healing account consisted of four verses or six, and that it was subsequently elaborated through other material. It turns out apparently to have consisted of the five-verse account which is found in Mark (8:22–26); and the other material is largely from Mark's accompanying context (Mark 8:11–21; 8:27–9:8).

The process of synthesizing texts—a technique which is found in both Jewish and Greco-Roman circles—provides a further partial precedent for what John has done. In the process of elaborately rewriting Mark's brief account he has, in effect, formed a unified synthesis of the surrounding Markan material.

The Intrinsic Similarity of the Texts

The similarities cover a wide range:

Theme. Both texts deal with essentially the same theme, that of increasing vision, especially that of increasing vision with regard to Jesus. And both set the development of that theme against the background of the Pharisees' misguidedness.

Position. Both texts stand at the center of their respective gospels.

Order. Apart from one change, John's main sequence of scenes follows that of Mark. In simplified outline:

| The Pharisees | The healing |
| The discussion | The discussion |

The healing	The Pharisees
The Christ	The Christ
The cost of discipleship	The cost of discipleship
Jesus revealed as divine	Jesus is worshipped

Details. Within each of John's scenes the similarities include details which in varying degrees are unique. The main items, scene by scene:

1. The Pharisees. "The Pharisees" speak of signs: apart from John 11:47, unique in Mark and John.
2. The discussion. The discussion's form: unique in Mark and John.
3. The healing. The details of the healing: apart from one element in Mark 7:33, four details are unique in the gospels, two of them unique in the NT.
4. The Christ. The (implied) revelation of Jesus as prophet and Christ is brought about by questioning people: unique in Mark and John.
5. The cost of discipleship. The idea of willing (*thelō*) to become a disciple: apart from the reuse of Mark's phrase by Matthew and Luke, unique in the NT.
6. Jesus is revealed/worshipped. Successive references to Moses: apart from three other instances, unique in Mark and John. Moses as involved in a heavenly conversation (*laleō*): apart from reuse of Mark by Matthew and Luke, unique in the NT.

The Consistency and Reasonableness of the Differences

The processes invoked to explain the considerable differences between the texts do not consist of unpredictable twistings and turnings, at odds with one another and with common sense. Rather, as already indicated, most of them may be accounted for through a few initial strategies (following Mark's main outline, dispersing and synthesizing, rewriting elaborately) and above all by four basic processes of adaptation— clarification, synthesizing, down-to-earth application, and focusing on the present. Together these four form a unity. They are all part of a single and coherent process of focusing the gospel as clearly and simply as possible on the here-and-now. It is a process which is not only reasonable in itself, but it is one which also accords with the basic idea, set forth by John at the beginning of his gospel, of the Word becoming flesh and dwelling among us (John 1:14).

Conclusion

It seems reasonable to draw a straightforward conclusion. In composing chapter 9, John made systematic use of Mark 8:11–9:8. He gave a literary adaptation which accorded with his own theological principle that the Word had entered the very fabric of human life. This is the simple explanation which accounts for the data. If literary dependence were extrinsically implausible, or if major sections of 8:11–9:8 found no counterpart at all in chapter 9, or if there was no correspondence in detail, or if the pattern of dissimilarities was jumbled or meaningless, then one would rightly hesitate to conclude that John systematically reworked the Markan text. But on none of these fronts is there any significant obstacle. The evidence concurs in pointing to direct literary dependence.

It does not, however, seem reasonable to say that the relationship between the texts is due to oral tradition. There is no known process of oral tradition—not even in the wide diversity evoked by the suggestions of Bultmann, Dodd, Gerhardsson and Kelber—which is capable of transforming a text in a way that is so complex and coherent. It is the literary explanation, and the literary explanation alone, which can account for the data.

8

John's Systematic Use of All of Mark

An Outline
(Rather Than a Proof) of One Aspect

The most essential clue to unravelling John's way of using Mark is provided in broad terms by Brown (45): "One of John's techniques is to show that themes occurring in one place in the Synoptics had a reality throughout the whole of Jesus' ministry." This observation was meant in a general way rather than as a statement that John actually used the synoptics, yet it encompasses a key insight: generally speaking, John does not reproduce the Markan episodes one by one; instead he divides them into aspects and disperses them so that they occur in a number of places. Elsewhere Brown (1961) has articulated this idea more clearly; he speaks of "incidents that are units in the synoptic gospels but dispersed in St. John."

An example of this procedure has already been seen in the reworking of the various episodes of Mark 8:11–9:8 (cf. John 9). John did not reproduce the Markan episodes one by one; instead he divided them according to varied aspects or viewpoints and then dispersed them throughout the chapter. Thus the actual healing, instead of being a single brief event (as in Mark 8:22–26) is referred to a number of times throughout the chapter. Likewise the Pharisees: instead of being initial background (cf. Mark 8:11–13) they are woven in and out of the whole story.

John's use of this process—this principle of dispersal and synthesis—may suggest that it is impossible to unravel his use of Mark as a whole;

such a principle allows for too much criss-crossing of texts, with all that such a criss-crossing implies by way of unpredictable variations and subtle blendings. To some degree this is true; the full extent of John's reworking of Mark will probably never be recovered.

Yet one of the central features of the relationship between Mark 8:11–9:8 and John 9 is that, despite the process of dispersal, despite the formulation of a whole new drama, John manages to preserve the essential order of the Markan episodes. He does not, of course, preserve them intact; each episode has been stripped of some of its aspects and has been rebuilt anew with the help of others. But he preserves enough of the episodes that, with an appropriate blend of disciplined imagination and patience, one can detect the central continuity.

It is on this central continuity—the fact that John, as a whole, preserves the essential order of *all* the Markan episodes—that the present chapter seeks to focus. Generally it does not try to explain or even suggest what John has done with the entirety of a particular text of Mark, with all its aspects. Instead, as the subtitle of the chapter suggests, it concentrates on just one aspect—that aspect of the various Johannine texts which in some form reflects the corresponding Markan text. It is as though, in dealing with Mark 8:11–9:8, the analysis in the preceding chapter had not attempted to trace what John had done with the several aspects of each Markan episode—how they were interwoven with one another—but had limited itself simply to showing that each of the six episodes in Mark 8:11–9:8 has a counterpart among the six episodes of John 9—and roughly in the same order.

Even within this focus, this concentration on one aspect, the analysis is not complete. What is generally provided is not so much a proof as simply an outline, an initial indication, sometimes tentative, of the persistent continuity between the two gospels.

It is important, therefore, in reading and assessing this chapter not to look for what it does not attempt to provide—systematic proof. Proof, insofar as it is possible in these matters, has been provided in dealing with the story of the blind man (John 9 and Mark 8:11–9:8). That is the episode which shows, as it were, that there's gold in them there hills. The present chapter, however, instead of mining deeply, is like an aerial photograph, an overview which, with varying degrees of clarity, indicates where others might make further finds.

For the reader therefore this is the end of the paved road, and it will not resume until chapter 13. The idea of an aerial photograph applies not only here (chapter 8, concerning John and Mark) but also to the following chapters (chapters 9–12, concerning John's relationship to Matthew, Luke-Acts, the Pentateuch and Ephesians respectively). Hence many readers will find it useful, on the first reading of this book, to skim these five chapters (particularly 8 and 9) and to move quickly to chapter 13. Afterwards one may come back to these chapters and look at them in detail, checking, refining, correcting, developing—and eventually laying down a smooth road for another generation.

The Outline

Each gospel (Mark and John) has been divided into nineteen sections—the division is pragmatic and is not meant to suggest the structure of either document—and as is shown in Table 8.1, the two may be placed side by side.

For pragmatic reasons the table gathers the nineteen sections into two major groups, A and B, and subdivides A and B into two lesser groups. Thus the nineteen sections are divided into four groups (1–5, 6–9, 10–12, 13–19). Generally each Markan text finds its Johannine partner within its own group. (Number 15, which involves Mark 13:5–23 and John 7:25–52, is an exception).

If however one were to pursue all the aspects of each Markan episode then one would find that very often texts do not stay within their own group; there is much greater freedom, much more complexity. The healing of the paralytic (Mark 2:1–12), for instance, involves at least two aspects—first the raising of a sick man (from sin and from his mat), and then a mild clash with the doubting scribes, with those who could not grasp the internal process which occurred when Jesus said, "Child, your sins are forgiven" (Mark 2:5). When John comes to this passage he duly incorporates it, and thus keeps Mark's order, but what he incorporates is just one aspect—the clash with the narrow mind (scribal/literary but unspiritual)—and he uses this, along with other material (especially concerning Gamaliel, Acts 5:17–42) to fill out the story of Nicodemus. As for the first aspect, the raising of the man from sin and his mat, John synthesizes this with aspects of later Markan texts, texts from another group—those dealing with increasingly bitter sabbath

Table 8.1. Mark as One Major Component of John:
A Tentative Outline of One Aspect

Section A	
Mark 1–6	John 1–6
1. Beginnings (including four disciples) (1:1–20).	Beginnings (including four disciples) (1:1–44).
	A fifth disciple, Nathanael (1:45–51).
2. The kingdom preached (1:21–39).	The kingdom symbolized (Cana) (2:1–11).
3. The cleansing of the leper (1:40–45).	The cleansing of the temple (2:12–22).
4. Healing: controversy with scribes (2:1–12).	Rebirth: controversy with Nicodemus (2:23–3:21).
5. A fifth disciple, Levi (2:13–17).	
6. John's disciples; the groom (2:18–22).	John's disciples, the groom (3:22–36).
	The Samaritan, sick son (chap. 4).
7. Sabbath controversy, healing (2:23–3:6).	Healing, sabbath controversy (chap. 5).
8. Multitudes, the seed (word), the sea (3:7–chap. 4), bread, the sea (6:30–56).	Multitudes, bread (wisdom), the sea (chap. 6).
9. The demoniac, sick daughter, etc. (5:1–6:29).	

controversies (Mark 2:23–3:6). And it is through this synthesizing of diverse aspects that he composes the account of the raising of the man at the pool (John 5:1–18).

The overall impression is that John seems to have absorbed and transformed the entire gospel of Mark. However startling at one level, such a conclusion can also be stated as if it were almost a platitude: in absorbing Mark, John did essentially what Matthew and Luke did, but he did it in his own way.

Examining the Outline: Aspects of an Analysis

The remainder of this chapter goes through the nineteen sections of Mark's gospel as found in the outline, and it offers indications that each

Section B

Mark 7–16	John 7–21
10. Clash with the Pharisees and departure for new regions (7:1–8:10).	Clash with the Jews; talk of departure; departure (chaps. 7–8). The revealing of the threatened Jesus as the Christ (7:25–52).
11. Advancing vision of Christ (8:11–9:8).	The man born blind (chap. 9).
?	The good shepherd (chap. 10).
12. Jesus talks of rising from the dead and raises the apparently dead boy (9:9–29).	The raising of Lazarus (11:1–44).
13. Teaching: the way, etc. (9:30–chap. 10).	
14a. Entry to Jerusalem, etc. (chap. 11).	Plot, anointing, entry to Jerusalem (11:45–12:19).
13b. Teaching: the vineyard, etc. (chap. 12).	
15. The stressful revealing of the Christ (13:5–23).	
16. The future revealing of the Son of humanity (13:1–4, 24–37).	Present revelation of the Son of humanity (12:20–50).
14b. Plot, anointing (14:1–9).	
17. Judas, the meal, denials (14:10–31).	The meal, Judas, denials (chap. 13). Teaching: the way, the vine, etc. (chaps. 14–16).
18. Final painful prayer (14:32–42).	Final ascentlike prayer (chap. 17).
19. Passion, resurrection (14:43–chap. 16).	Passion, resurrection (chaps. 18–21).

section of Mark finds an equivalent in John. At times this chapter also refers to other texts, especially to Matthew. The extent of these indications varies considerably. The final section, for instance, concerning the passion narratives (Mark 14:45–chap. 16, John 18–21) could have been the subject of extensive analysis. But the passion accounts are not a problem, at least not in the same way, for it is in these final chapters, rather than in any other part of the gospel, that it is easy to see that, despite their many differences, the two gospels are dealing with essentially the same events. Thus scarcely any analysis is offered.

The purpose then is not to provide a full analysis, or anything like it.

On the contrary, the various comments have a very limited goal: to show that, when one *begins* to analyze the texts, one encounters repeated indications that John systematically transformed Mark or, at least, indications that such a process of transformation is worthy to be considered as a useful working hypothesis.

Section A: From the Easy Beginnings to the Miracles of Bread and Water (Mark 1–6, John 1–6)

1. Beginnings (Mark 1:1–20; John 1:1–44)

The affinities between these texts may be summarized in Table 8.2. John's text involves both other sources and another purpose, yet he has made systematic use of Mark.

In place of Mark's opening summary sentence (1:1: "The beginning [*archē*] of the gospel of Jesus Christ . . ."), John has introduced an elaborate prologue (1:1–18). Integrated into that prologue is a distillation of Mark's picture of John the baptizer (Mark 1:4–8), a distillation in which—following one of the themes of the fourth gospel—the baptizer is seen primarily as a preacher or witness (John 1:6, 15).

Unlike Mark, the fourth evangelist does not describe Jesus as being baptized and tempted; such ideas would not fit well with the exalted picture of Jesus as descending from God. Instead the baptism account is so rewritten that it exalts Jesus above John, and the picture of a temptation or trial is adapted to become the trial-like questioning of John.

Table 8.2.

Mark 1:1–20	John 1:1–44
The beginning; John's preaching (1:1–8).	The prologue (including John) (1:1–18).
Jesus' baptism; the Spirit descends (1:9–11).	John is questioned/tried (1:19–28).
Jesus' temptation/trial (1:12–13).	John baptizes; the Spirit descends on Jesus (1:29–34).
Jesus' preaches the kingdom/realm of God and calls four disciples (1:14–20).	Jesus invites disciples to his abode; the calling of four disciples (1:35–44).

In comparison with Mark's brief temptation account (1:12–13) the description of the questioning of John is quite elaborate (John 1:19–28). This elaboration rests not only on the inclusion of some of Mark's earlier quotation from Isaiah (". . . the voice of one crying . . ."; Mark 1:2–3; cf. John 1:23), but especially on the elaboration which had already been wrought on Mark by Matthew. John apparently has taken Matthew's account of a three-part temptation by the devil (Matt 4:1–13) and turned it into a three-part questioning by the emissaries of the Jews (John 1:19–23). As in reworking Mark 8:11–9:8 (especially the transfiguration), John's adaptation is thoroughly down to earth; he takes a rather exotic account and integrates into it normal human experience. Yet the essence of the trial remains the same—the problem of answering "Who are you?" (Matt 4:3, 6: "If you are. . . . If you are . . ."; John 1:19: "Who are you?"). In each text, three false possibilities are put forward, and all three are rejected.

The later part of the trial scene, when John seems to refer to an apocalyptic expectation of an unknown Messiah (John 1:24–27, ". . . there is one among you whom you do not know;" cf. Brown, 53) would seem to be a distillation of the idea, taken from John's preaching, that the coming of Christ involves an impending process of harvesting and burning (Mark 1:7–8 and especially Matt 3:10–12: "Already the axe is laid to the root . . ."). Again the picture given in the fourth gospel is much less spectacular, but again the essential idea is the same—in this case that the coming of Christ involves a fundamental disruption of set ways of thinking and doing.

In reworking Mark's account of the first preaching (1:14–15) and of the first disciples (1:16–20) John has made several changes. Jesus enters the stage not as a preacher of the kingdom but as someone who in the course of normal human existence—he is pictured simply as walking—abides with God (in the Spirit: John 1:36–38).

The first disciples correspondingly are pictured not as preachers—the imagery of fishing and of being fishers of people is left aside and will not be used until John 21—but as people who follow this person who is walking and as people who seek the place where he abides. Thus the notion of the realm (kingdom) of God is maintained, but the emphasis on abiding suggests that the essence of that realm is within, in a steady dynamic of togetherness in the spirit.

This realm, however, is not confined to what is within. The very first result of the abiding is that Andrew goes and tells his brother, Peter

(John 1:41). This is hardly preaching, yet it is the process on which preaching rests.

Unlike Mark, John puts considerable emphasis on Jesus' naming of Peter (1:40–42)—an elaboration which, given John's other adaptations of Matthew, would seem to be a reworking of part of the scene at Caesarea Philippi in which Jesus named Peter and proclaimed him to be the foundation rock of the church (Matt 16:18). The difference in John is that even though Peter is important—his name dominates John 1:40–42—he is not the foundation of the disciples being together; the foundation consists of the shared abiding in the Spirit.

2. The First Miracle(s): the Kingdom of God Is Like the Outpouring of a New Spirit (Mark 1:21–39, John 2:1–11)

Having announced the approach of the kingdom of God (Mark 1:14–15), Jesus proceeds to inaugurate it and to inaugurate it abundantly. In an intense journey of teaching, preaching, and prayer, a journey which takes him all through Galilee, he is revealed as the Holy One, the one who comes from God and who combats every form of evil—first of all, an unclean spirit, and then, fever, diseases, and devils (Mark 1:21–39). In John, however, there is no such account; the entire dramatic journey, with all its implications of a profound impact on Galilee, is never described. Instead there is the account of the wedding feast at Cana (2:1–11).

Yet, there are curious links between the two texts. A. Maynard (1985) has indicated, for instance, that Mark's first miracle, with its "What is there to us and to you" (1:24) provides a partial precedent for Cana, particularly for its "What is there to me and to you" (John 2:4). What is especially significant is that both of these opening miracles are essentially concerned with the inbreaking of God's holy Spirit. In Mark it is stated implicitly and negatively: God's Holy One drives out the spirit that is unclean. In John it is implicit but positive: the pouring forth of the surpassing wine, a wine associated with Jesus' hour and with obedience to his word, is an intimation of the granting of the Spirit.

Furthermore, without attempting a complete analysis, the texts as a whole (Mark 1:21–39; John 2:1–11) show several other points of contact:

The power of Jesus' commanding word (Mark 1:25–26; John 2:5).
Subsequent surprise (Mark 1:27, John 2:9–10).
A woman, and service/servants (Mark 1:30–31, John 2:5).
Intimations of raising people/resurrection (Mark 1:31, 35; John 2:1:
"on the third day . . .").
A sense of something secret (Mark 1:24, 34; John 2:9).
A sense of Jesus' making a fundamental breakthrough in the process
of revealing himself and of evoking belief (Mark 1:28, 37; John
2:11).

For a comparison of Mark's kingdom, which implies a new kind of
Spirit, and John's kindgomlike wedding, which symbolizes the coming
Spirit, see Table 8.3.

What John apparently has done is taken Mark's initial account of
Jesus' revealing the kingdom and synthesized it into the single image of
Jesus' (described as a king in John 1:49) revealing the fine wedding
wine. Such an image is not alien; it corresponds to a major element in
the description of the kingdom as being like a wedding feast (Matt
22:1–14). Thus, in much the same way that John took the Markan
account of the calling of the first apostles and rewrote it in conjunction
with the later Matthean account of the naming of Peter, he has now
taken the initial Markan picture of the revealing of the kingdom and
transformed it in light of the later Matthean parable. The essence of the
Markan text is maintained but it has been adapted to the imagery of the
wedding wine. And an important part of the Matthean parable has also
been kept—but in a form that is less parabolic, closer to human experience.

Table 8.3.

Mark 1:21–39, The First Miracles	John 2:1–11, The First Miracle
Expelling the unclean spirit (1:21–28). Sick woman is raised, serves (1:29–34). Jesus rises, prays, and preaches (1:35–39).	Amid suggestions of resurrection (hour, third day), with help from the woman and servants, Jesus brings an abundance of new wine/Spirit (2:1–11).

3. The Cleansing of the Temple of the Body (Mark 1:40–45, John 2:12–22)

At this point Mark tells of the cleansing of the leper (1:40–45), and John of the cleansing of the temple (2:12–22). The two are obviously very different, and the clearest ingredient in John's text is not from the beginning of Mark (concerning the leper) but from near the end of the gospel—from Mark's own account of the cleansing of the temple (11:15–17; cf. Matt 21:12–13).

However, the brief synoptic description of the cleansing of the temple (two or three verses) does not account for John's longer text; the fourth evangelist has used other sources.

Among these other sources one was the cleansing of the leper—not all of it, but one aspect of it. Already, in composing the previous (Cana) text, he appears to have used a further aspect of it, one which involved the explicit use of the word *katharismos*, "cleansing" (Mark 1:44, John 2:6—apart from John 3:25, the word does not otherwise occur in either gospel). Now he returns to the cleansing and he takes from it an aspect or viewpoint which shows Jesus as going through two stages: one in which he is supremely in command (he *wills* the leprosy away, Mark 1:40–42; he drives out the money-lenders, John 2:12–17), and the second in which he is more humanly involved, more vulnerable and subject to human limitations, more engaged with evil (he displays emotion to the man and tells him to show himself to the priest, Mark 1:43–44; he responds to the questioning Jews by alluding to their destruction of him—"Destroy this sanctuary," John 2:18–21).

In Mark, the cleansing is that of a body. In John, it is that of a temple, but as the account develops, "temple" gives way to "sanctuary," meaning body.

4. Jesus Knows the Thoughts of the Unspiritual Scribes/Pharisee and Mildly Confronts Them/Him with God's Life–Giving Power (Mark 2:1–12, Healing the Paralytic; John 2:23–3:21, Nicodemus)

As already noted, when John is reworking Mark 2:1–12, he uses its central healing account as part of the poolside incident (John 5:1–18), and what he incorporates here is its other main aspect—that of a confrontation with those who are learned but unspiritual (the scribes, Nicodemus).

A further detail may be added. In Mark (2:8), Jesus is described as knowing what is in the scribes' hearts. In John, Nicodemus is introduced as a human being (*anthrōpos*), and thus as one of those concerning whom it was said that Jesus knew what was in them (2:23–3:1). Thus he knows what is in the unspiritual, but they have almost no idea of God, of how God can give new life.

5. The Call of a Fifth Disciple: Levi (Matthew), and Nathanael (Mark 2:13–17, John 1:45–51)

Both Mark and John record the call of a fifth disciple, someone who to some degree is outside the initial group or pattern. The call of Levi (Mark 2:13–17) is distinct from that of the initial four (1:16–20), and the call of Nathanael (John 1:45–51), though joined with John's initial four, stands out in a number of ways.

A central feature of both of these later calls, and one which is quite absent from the call of the initial four, is a sense that the person has been living in a state of alienation, sinfulness. It is in describing the call of Levi that Mark first uses the word "sinner," and he uses it four times. In the case of Nathanael the word "sinner" does not occur but, as examination of 1:45–51 indicates, a state of pessimism and alienation is implied. The fig tree, for instance, under which Nathanael had been standing, evokes the trees and fig leaves under which the fallen couple in Genesis had tried to hide.

Yet both Mark and John have integrated this late call into that of the original four—Mark by recalling the sea (2:13), the scene of the call of the initial four (1:16), and John by weaving the Nathanael account into the account of the others.

6. John's Disciples, the Groom, and the Associate(s) of the Groom: the Difficult Transition from the Old Order to the New (Mark 2:18–22, John 3:22–36)

When there is an apparent problem about the contrast between the fasting practice of John's disciples and the more relaxed practice of Jesus' own disciples, Jesus uses the metaphor of a wedding: he is the groom, and those with him are like a groom's attendants; a new order has begun (Mark 2:18–22).

In the fourth gospel (3:22–36), when John's disciples, having become involved in a dispute about cleansing, complain to him about Jesus, John too uses the metaphor of a wedding: Jesus is the groom, and he, John, is simply the groom's friend—one who steps aside to make room for the new heavenly order. Thus the fourth gospel retains the basic image of the groom who introduces the new order, but the other elements have been adapted considerably.

7. Sabbath Controversy and Healing (Mark 2:23– 3:6, John 5)

First the Pharisees tell Jesus that plucking grain on the sabbath "is not lawful" (Mark 2:23–28), and when on the sabbath he raises up and heals the man with the withered hand, they go out and plot to kill him (Mark 3:1–6).

In John 5:1–18 Jesus' raising up and healing of the sick man on the sabbath is following first by the accusation that what he has done "is not lawful" and then by a desire to kill him.

As already noted, in this case it is reasonably easy to detect one of the supplemental sources—the healing of the parlytic (Mark 2:1–12).

As for John's subsequent discourse (5:19–47) Mark provides little support for it. However, attached to Matthew's version of the sabbath controversies (in the cornfields and in the synagogue) there are some elaborations, and it is these passages, along with a text from Matthew 23, as shown in Table 8.4, which provide initial clues as to the origin of John's text.

The similarity of John's glory-seeking passage (5:41–47) to that of

Table 8.4.

Matthew 11, 12, 23	John 5:19–47
Witness (by John) and refusal (11:1–24)	
God of creation, Father, Son (11:25–30).	Creation, Father, Son, judgment
Sabbath controversies (12:1–14).	(5:19–29).
The beloved gives true judgment (12:15–21).	
	Witnesses and refusal (5:30–40).
The scribes seek glory (23:1–12).	The Jews seek glory (5:41–47).

Matthew 23 is fairly clear, and has been indicated by Brown (229). But Brown (216–17) also links John 5 with Matthew 12, and it is by following that lead that one comes to the overall importance of Matthew 11 and 12, and especially to the pivotal role of the poetic exclamation concerning the parentlike God of creation (Matt 11:25–30). This is the text which, more than any other, underlies the discourse of John 5.

8. God's Realm Comes to People, People's Diverse Reactions (Mark 3:7–chap. 4, 6:30–56, John 6)

On either side of Mark 5:1–6:29 lie two narrative blocks which, though separated, are in some ways related. The first consists of almost two chapters (3:7–chap. 4) and deals largely with *people* (the multitude, the twelve, and the relatives and scribes—3:7–35), with *parables* (4:1–34), and with the *storm at sea* (4:35–41). The second, which is considerably shorter (6:30–56), speaks of the *loaves* (6:30–44), of *walking on the sea* (6:45–52), and of the many *people* who recognized Jesus and were healed (6:53–56). Thus some of the elements of the first block reappear in the second, but in a form that is varied or developed.

The largest single section in these two blocks is the series of parables (4:1–34). This parabolic section, as well as being large, is striking—a colorful new way of speaking of God's word and God's realm. Yet prominent though it is, it is not mentioned in John. (See Table 8.5.)

The puzzle begins to be resolved when account is taken of "the Johannine technique of replacing 'the kingdom of God is like . . . ' with 'I am . . . '" (Brown, 670). In other words, instead of parables John tends to give some form of "I am . . ." discourse.

The discourse in this case is about the bread of life (John 6:25–59, esp. 6:25–51). John has taken the various parables and synthesized them into a flowing unity. Thus instead of the many ways in which the seed is not received (Mark 4:1–20) he gives the down-to-earth picture of people actually failing to perceive or accept the bread (see esp. John 6:25–31). And instead of saying that the realm of God is like diverse seeds which give life and shelter (Mark 4:26–32), he speaks of himself as the bread which provides both life and a place to which people may come (John 6:34–51).

As in previous instances, John has not only synthesized the diverse items in Mark; he has also filtered them through a new kind of imagery—in this case the imagery of bread.

Table 8.5.

Mark 3:7–chap. 4; 6:30–56	John 6
The multitude (3:7–12).	*The multitude* (6:1–2; cf 5:3).
The twelve (3:13–19). The relatives (3:20–35): no bread; Jesus counters Satan-related reactions (3:20–27); spirit, not flesh/family (3:28–35).	
Parables concerning seed (the seed symbolizes the word), Storm at sea (4:1–41).	*Loaves, stormy sea, crossing* (6:3–24).
Loaves, sea, crossing, etc. (6:30–56).	*A discourse on bread* (the bread symbolizes wisdom) (6:25–59).
	Jesus counters negative reactions, esp. by emphasizing Spirit, not flesh. Reaction of *the twelve,* one of whom is a devil (6:60–71).

The selection of this image is understandable. Seed by its very nature often grows into wheat and thus into bread. Furthermore in the later block (Mark 6:30–56) bread is the leading image. John has taken that image and used it as a way of interpreting the parable.

The result (John 6) is a chapter which begins with the bread and with the incidents which follow it (the sea crossing and the people's receptiveness: John 6:3–24; cf. Mark 6:30–56) and which then goes on with the discourse on the bread of life.

John has also used the references to various groups of people (Mark 3:7–35). The opening picture of the multitude (Mark 3:7–12) has helped to form John's opening picture (6:1–2). And the subsequent pictures, of the twelve and of the relatives (Mark 3:13–19 and 3:20–35), have helped to form John's conclusion (6:60–71). The transformation in this final text is quite radical. As is suggested by the outline, John has taken the incident involving the relatives, including the intervening discussion concerning Satan (Mark 3:20–35) and has used it to speak of the negative reactions to his discourse. The contrast between spirit and flesh (cf. the relatives), which in Mark is merely implied obscurely, in John is stated explicitly. And the fight against Satan, instead of being located in an obscure discussion about Beelzeboul, is placed in down-to-earth human reality, right among the twelve.

John 6, as well as using Mark 3:7–4:41 and 6:30–56, depends also on other texts. Thus the final part of the discourse, for instance, when Jesus speaks of eating his flesh and drinking his blood (John 6:52–58) is generally seen as containing John's rendition of the eucharistic texts (cf. Mark 14:22–25, Matt 26:26–39, Luke 22:17–20). Furthermore, Peter's acknowledgment of Jesus as the Holy One of God (John 6:68–69) is frequently regarded as being, in part, a variation on Peter's declaration of Jesus as the Christ (Mark 8:29, Matt 16:16). And the Jews' objections to Jesus (John 6:41–42) reflect something of Jesus' rejection at Nazareth (Mark 6:1–6).

In other ways also John 6 involves the combining of texts. Thus the walking on the water (6:16–21), though primarily dependent on the Mark/Matthew report of the same event (Mark 6:45–52, Matt 14:22–27), has drawn also on the account of the storm at sea (Mark 4:35–41). And the narrative concerning the multiplication of the loaves (John 6:1–13) is so written that it refers to both Jews and Gentiles—and thereby combines the essence of both the Markan multiplication accounts (6:30–44, 8:1–10).

What is essential—whatever the multiplicity of sources and however intricate the criss-crossing of details—is that in chapter 6 John's central affinity is with Mark 3:7–chap. 4 and 6:30–56. In place of Mark's diversity, obscurity and remoteness, John has rendered a version which, comparatively speaking, is unified, clear and down-to-earth. The realm of God is no longer explained in difficult parables. Instead it takes the form of an "I am . . ."—a phrase which, however divine in its connotations, is also immensely human. And the reaction of people to that realm, instead of being described in general terms, is depicted in a drama involving specific groups and individuals. Mark had spoken parabolically of the word. John implies practical wisdom—the word becoming flesh.

9. Setting People Free and Proclaiming the Message (the Gerasene Demoniac, etc.: Mark 5:1–6:29, the Samaritan Woman: John 4)

As Mark's gospel develops, some of its episodes become much more expansive. Thus in chapters 1–4 the various accounts are generally very short, but in chapters 5 and 6 (within 5:1–6:29) there are three stories which, both in length and in colorful human drama, break the mold—

the Gerasene demoniac (5:1–20), the story of Jairus's daughter and the sick woman (5:21–43), and the story of King Herod (6:14–29).

Essential to these stories is the idea of setting people free from their inner constrictions and weakness. This theme, of course, is not new in the gospel; it had been at the heart of Jesus' initial journey through Galilee (1:21–45). But now it is played out in human detail. The Gerasene demoniac, plagued by an unclean spirit, is finally freed from bondage. And the female figures also are released—the woman from an unnatural draining of her life, and the girl from premature death. Herod, however, would seem to be a contrast character. King though he is, and close as he is to the word, he does not receive it. On the contrary, his servitude intensifies. Having begun by being captive to Herodias, he continues by subjecting himself to her daughter. And instead of breaking free, he allows himself to be tied by his own foolish oath and by peer pressure. Thus he kills the one thing he knows to be good.

Amid these stories, between the second (the women) and the third (Herod), there are two brief episodes, which suggest an expanding horizon. On the one hand, Jesus' original base, at Nazareth, rejects him (Mark 6:1–6a), and on the other, he sends forth the twelve—essentially to do what he had already been doing and thus to expand and multiply his work (Mark 6:6b–13). The overall effect—three long stories gathered around an expanding horizon—is such that it suggests a major development in the form and content of the gospel.

In John, however, these major stories are never mentioned. Instead, there is the account of the Samaritan woman, a story which, in its length and content, stands out from all that precedes, and in the midst of which there is a discussion of an expanding mission. In this dramatic account, and in the brief episode which is joined to it (concerning the royal official's son: 4:43–54), John has once again synthesized the many Markan texts. In Mark, the drama of servitude was varied and exotic. In John, it is rendered into a form which is simpler and closer to human experience.

This does not mean that Mark's text accounts fully for John 4:1–42. There is far more in the story of the Samaritan woman than is found in the earlier gospel. The discussion of the mission (John 4:31–38), for instance, while partly inspired by Mark 6:1–13, draws also on other sources. Similarly, the story of the official's son; its positioning at this point is influenced by the account of Jairus's daughter, but it has a greater indebtedness to other texts, particularly to the similar account in Matt 8:5–13. Yet as is suggested in Table 8.6, Mark has been used.

Table 8.6.

Mark 5:1–6:29	John 4
The Gerasene demoniac (5:1–20). Jesus comes to the . . . Gerasenes. The unclean man meets him, . . . and worships. Initial antagonism towards Jesus.	*The Samaritan woman* (4:1–42). Jesus comes to Samaria. The woman comes for water. Initial antagonism towards Jesus.
Jesus expels the unclean spirits. Jesus heals the woman with the flow (*pēgē*) of blood (5:25–34).	To the woman who is weary of drawing water Jesus offers a flowing spring (*pēgē*) of water.
Herod's marriage situation and his captivity to the daughter, bring death (6:16–29).	The woman's inadequate series of relationships, within marriage and outside of it.
	The question of worship.
The herdsmen go, tell the city. From Nazareth to mission (6:1–13). The people come, ask Jesus to leave. The man spreads the word.	The woman goes, tells the city. Discussion of the mission. The people come, ask Jesus to stay. The woman had spread the word.
Jairus's daughter (5:21–24, 35–43). The rule of the synagogue, whose daughter was dying, asked him to come to her. They are met by news of death, but Jesus brings life.	*The official's son* (4:43–54). The royal official, whose son was about to die, asked him to come down. He is met by news of life, life given by Jesus.

The transformation which has been wrought on Mark 5:1–6:29 is rather like that which had been wrought earlier on the initial revealing of the kingdom (Mark 1:21–45). In that instance the Markan text had not only been synthesized, it had also been filtered through the imagery of a wedding feast (John 2:1–11). Here too the synthesized text is filtered— in this case through the imagery of a betrothal scene. (Literary analysis of Jesus' meeting with the woman at the well of Samaria, John 4:1–42, shows that it is a radical variation on the conventional biblical scene wherein a betrothal is initiated at a well in a foreign land. See Genesis 24 and 29, Exod 2:15–22. In John 4:1–42 the betrothal is not physical but spiritual.)

Apart from the betrothal framework, the next most important foundation text is the account of the Gerasene demoniac. Within Mark 5:1–6:29 this is the leading story and, as the above outline indicates, it is into this context that the other stories have been fitted.

Unlike the first Cana instance, however, John does not form all the Markan texts into a single episode. Instead he goes on to tell the distinct story of the official's son. Yet this story—again set in Cana—is integrated with the lengthy betrothal scene. Together the two episodes form a single journey, and, even though the final part of that journey deals with the threat of death, the larger part of the journey is concerned with the deepening of ongoing life.

An examination of the details and implications of John's transformation is not to be undertaken lightly and, therefore, is best left to further research. The issues raised in these stories, particularly in the agony of the forlorn unclean man and in the (complementary?) anguish of the woman whose life-blood is draining away, reach into the depths of the human soul and spirit, and into a perception of human existence as being mired in dread and decay. Yet Mark turns that perception around, showing the presence of a saving power, and John turns it yet more, indicating that the apparent disintegration of life can be the starting point for bringing everything together in a betrothal with God.

Section B: From Confronting Jewish Tradition/Law to Descending into Death (Mark 7–16, John 7–21)

At this point Mark's text (Mark 7:1–9:8) suggests, among other things, a departure from Jewish tradition. In 7:1–23 the Pharisees are confronted, and in 8:11–13 they are left behind. At the same time there is an implication of new horizons, an implication which reaches its fullest in the transfiguration. Thus the departure which is entailed in the confrontation is something positive, forward-looking.

But what follows, after the transfiguration, is essentially a journey down to death. At the beginning of Mark 9 Jesus is on a mountain, but already in 9:9 he is on the way down, and his subsequent journey will not cease until, just before his arrest, he comes to Gethsemane and, facing death, falls to the ground (14:32–42).

Peter, James, and John do not understand this downward journey, either at its height or in its depths. At its height, coming down from the mountain, they do not understand the meaning of rising from the dead (9:9–13). And when faced by the man whose son falls to the ground and then apparently dies (9:14–29, esp. vv 20, 26, 27, 29), they and the rest of the disciples seem incapable of the kind of prayer that would have confronted that death. At the journey's depths, in Gethsemane, when it is Jesus who is on the ground, they are equally incapable.

What is important is that the two meetings with death (in Mark 9:9–29 and in 14:32–42) form a certain unity. The disciples, for the moment, may not have the necessary spirit of prayer to enter fully into the mysterious struggle, but on the mountain they had caught a glimpse of something beyond ordinary life, and in Jesus there is a power greater than death—a power which shows itself already in the raising of the one who seems to be dead, and which will be seen again when, with a kind of spiritual revitalization, he goes forward to confront his own death (14:42).

Hence even though Mark 9:9–14:42 is a journey towards death, death does not govern that journey. There may be many reminders of mortality—such as the predictions of death (9:30–32, 10:32–34) and the anointing (14:8)—but the essential picture, from beginning to end, is one of profound vitality.

It is these texts (Mark 7:1–9:8 and 9:9–14:42) which John uses as major components for chapters 7 to 17. First, the sense of confronting Jewish tradition and departing from it (as in Mark 7:1–9:8) is reflected, but with greater clarity, in John 7 10.

Second, the sense of a journey towards death (Mark 9:9–14:42) is used in composing chapters 11 to 17. In John's account also, as in Mark 9:9–14:42, death threatens powerfully—from the striking down of Lazarus to the time when it is announced repeatedly that Jesus' own hour has come (12:23, 13:1, 17:1), an hour in which he will be like a grain of wheat which falls to the ground and dies (12:23–24).

10. Clash with the Pharisees/Jews, and (Talk of) Departure, Especially to the Greeks/Gentiles (Mark 7:1–8:10, John 7–8)

The extensive Markan text (7:1–8:10) may be divided into two sections of roughly equal length—the clash with Jewish traditions (7:1–23), and the departure for a life-giving journey to places that are foreign or unknown (7:24–8:10: healing both the daughter of the Greek Syrophoenician woman and also the deaf man of Decapolis; then supplying bread and going to Dalmanutha). The overall effect of these two contrasting sections is to suggest a departure from a tradition which is confined and shallow to one which breaks boundaries and gives life. This basic idea—a departure from narrow Judaism to something more life-giving—seems to have provided one component for John 7–8. In these chapters the text moves from an initial clash with the Jews (esp. in John 7:14–24) to various ideas about departure (7:33–36, 8:21–22) and to an acute sense of the contrast between Jesus, who is life-giving and grounded in God (cf. esp. 7:37–39; 8:12–30, 56–58) and "the Jews" (focused on death and grounded in the devil; cf. esp. 8:21, 39–44).

The fact that Mark 7:1–8:10 provided one component does not mean that it was used in its entirety within John 7–8; aspects of it seem to have been used in other Johannine texts. Thus the picture of the Syrophoenician woman coming to Jesus may, perhaps, have contributed something to John's description of the woman of Samaria (4:1–42), and—more easy to detect—the "opening" of the deaf man (7:35) is reflected in the "opening" of the eyes of the man born blind (John 9:10, 14, 17, 21, 26, 30, 32). Furthermore, the supplying of bread, insofar as it suggests a care which is universal (*seven* loaves, *seven* baskets, *four* thousand: Mark 8:6–10) has contributed to the universal emphasis of John's multiplication account (6:1–13).

Having made these qualifications—that Mark 7:1–8:10 supplies only one component, and that not all of the Markan text is used within John 7–8—it is now possible to focus on the essence of the connection, or at least on part of it as shown in Table 8.7.

In both gospels these texts give the first major explicit clashes concerning the quality of Jewish observance of God's commandment/law. They are also the first texts to employ any form of the word "Greek."

11. Advancing Vision (Mark 8:11–9:8, John 9)

See chapter 7, above.

12. The Idea of Rising from the Dead, and the Actual Raising of Someone Who Appears Dead (Mark 9:9–29, John 11:1–44)

It has been indicated by K. Pearce (1985) that John's story of Lazarus uses several Lukan texts as a springboard, especially the account of the

Table 8.7.

Mark	John
The clash regarding tradition (7:1–23). Empty Jewish teachings forget God's commandment and teach human tradition (7:1–8).	*The clash regarding the law* (7:15–24). The teaching of Jesus is not based on human learning but on God (7:14–18).
Jewish tradition nullifies the word of God (7:9–13).	The Jews do not maintain the law; they seek to kill Jesus (7:19–20).
Jewish tradition, preoccupied with externals, does not understand the importance of what is within (7:14–23).	Do not judge by appearances, but judge just judgement (7:24).
Departure to foreign lands (7:25). Jesus is met by the woman who was *Hellēnis,* lit. "Greek."	*Talk of departure* (7:35). The Jews ask if Jesus will go to teach the *Hellēnas,* "Greeks."

raising of the widow's son (Luke 7:11–17; cf. Lazarus in Luke 16:19–31). To some degree this appears to be true, though one needs to ask whether John used all of Luke-Acts or just a part of it (see Appendix D). In any case, such use of Luke does not exclude the dependence of the Lazarus story on Mark, in this case Mark's account of how Jesus first discussed the idea of rising from the dead (9:9–13) and then went on actually to raise up someone who appeared dead (9:14–29). Mark's text has aspects of an exorcism, and, as always, these are omitted by John. What he has retained, and enhanced, is a dramatic victory over apparent death, a victory which is an indication of how he will eventually deal with his own death. Among the links between the main texts (Mark 9:9–29, John 11:1–44) the following may be noted:

At first (Mark 9:9–13, John 11:1–16) Jesus and the disciples are at some distance from the scene of encroaching death. (In Mark they are coming down from the mountain. In John they are leaving their previous abode and going toward Lazarus). Jesus speaks confidently but sometimes rather obscurely about implied resurrection and restoration, but the disciples cannot grasp the mysterious process.

Then (Mark 9:14–24, John 11:17–37) there is a prolonged scene in which, when Jesus arrives, he becomes involved not so much with the central figure (the son who falls to the ground, the dead Lazarus) as with the relatives—the father in Mark, the two sisters in John. The key issue in this discussion is that of believing. The father goes through a difficult process of trying to advance from unbelief to believing. In John the distinction between belief and unbelief is clarified dramatically in the contrast between the two sisters. Mark's picture of the destructive force of the negative spirit has been omitted by John and seems to be replaced by the implication that there is some kind of battle going on within the spirit of Jesus (cf. Mark 9:17,18,20; John 11:33).

In the third scene (Mark 9:25–29, John 11:38–44) Jesus confronts directly the one who seems to be dead. Something of the previous spiritual battle is renewed (Mark 9:25–26, John 11:38), and the person seems hopelessly dead, but by means of prayer, implied or spoken, Jesus' words bring the person back to life.

By and large John's text is much clearer. It is not immediately obvious, for instance, in Mark, that the discussion concerning resurrection on the way down from the mountain introduces the subsequent drama of death and life. But John, in reworking the material, has integrated it fully.

Apart from Mark 9:9–29, the story of Lazarus seems to have made partial use of the Matthean texts concerning Jesus' return (24:45–chap. 25) and concerning the plot to kill him (26:1–5, esp. vv 3–5; cf. Mark 14:1–2). In particular the motif of the delayed return and the image of the diverse maidens as coming to meet the returning Lord, appear to have contributed significantly to John's picture of Jesus' delayed return and to the portrayal of Martha and Mary.

Matthew then goes on, almost immediately, to tell briefly of the meeting, held in the courtyard of Caiaphas, which decided to kill Jesus (26:3–5). And at the end of the Lazarus story John tells, more elaborately, of a similar Caiaphas-inspired meeting (11:45–53).

13. Jesus Teaches Concerning the Way and the Vine (Mark 9:30–chap. 10, chap. 12; John 14–16??)

Following his proleptic involvement with death (Mark 9:9–29), Jesus goes on to deliver two necklacelike teaching sessions. The image of the necklace—often used of Mark—expresses the fact that the texts in question are composed of passages which are small and not clearly interrelated. The first such text extends in effect from Galilee to Jerusalem (9:30–10:52), and despite the variety of its many pieces, it is governed in large part by a single image—that of journeying or following a way (*hodos*: cf. 9:30, 33; 10:1, 17, 21, 32, 46, 52). The second text consists of chapter 12, and it is set entirely in Jerusalem (it follows the various entrances of chapter 11 and precedes the exit to the Mountain of Olives: 13:1, 2). Its dominating image, insofar as it has one, is that which is conveyed by the parable of the vineyard (12:1–12).

The proposal which is made here, and made very tentatively, is that these two texts have been used, in part at least, in composing John 13–17, especially chapters 14–16. To a significant degree it is the image of a way (*hodos*) or of teaching a way (*hodegeō*), which sets the tone for John 14 and 16:4b–33 (cf. 14:4–6, 16:13). And in John 15:1–16:4a the leading image is that of the true vine.

Obviously within the two Markan texts, certain passages (or certain aspects of some passages) have greater affinity with texts other than the last discourse. The second and third passion predictions (Mark 9:30–32, 10:32–34), for instance, have a ready link with Jesus' second and third statements about the lifting up of the Son of humanity (John 8:28, 12:32–34). And the healing of the blind Bartimaeus, who once had sat and begged (Mark 10:46), has apparently contributed to John 9 (9:8). But in a last discourse which is so concerned with death and discipleship even the passion predictions and Bartimaeus may have a role.

14. Jesus Enters Jerusalem (Mark 11), the Plot and the Anointing (Mark 14:1–9, cf. John 11:45–12:19)

In Mark there is a wide gap (three chapters) between the entry to Jerusalem (chap. 11) and the anointing (chap. 14). Not so in John, as is shown in Table 8.8.

John has reversed the order in such a way that the anointing at Bethany is a prelude to Jesus entering Jerusalem, and also in such a way that all three episodes (including the plot) have been fully integrated into the larger plan of chapters 11 and 12, especially into the story of Lazarus. Thus the plot scene, so brief in Mark (14:1–2), has been expanded so that it forms an adequate final section to the Lazarus account (11:45–53). One element of this expansion was readily available to John—in Matthew's longer version of the same episode (Matt 26:1–5).

Mark 11 has a certain geographic unity: it begins with the image of nearing Jerusalem and then goes on to tell, three times, of Jesus "coming to Jerusalem"—first to be acclaimed and to look around at the

Table 8.8.

Mark 11:1–11; 14:1–9	John 11:45–12:19
Entry to Jerusalem (11:1–11).	
Plot (14:1–2; cf. Matt 26:1–5).	Plot (esp. because of Lazarus) (11:45–53).
Anointing (14:3–9).	Anointing (Lazarus present) (12:1–11).
	Entry (Lazarus a factor) (12:12–19).

temple (11:1–11, esp. v 11); next day, to curse the fig tree and cleanse the temple (11:12–19, esp. v 15); and again, on the following day, to comment on the withered tree and, in the temple, to meet a challenge to his authority (11:20–33, esp. v 27).

Some of this material has already been used by John—particularly in the account of Jesus cleansing the temple and being challenged by the Jews (John 2:12–18). And the withered tree (Mark 11:12–14, 20–25)—a symbol apparently for the withered faith of the Jews—may have been used in depicting the faithless brothers (John 7:3–8).

Thus the one major text in Mark 11 for which John thus far has had no equivalent is the initial episode—the triumphal entry (11:1–11). Now however, in 12:12–19, he uses it, adapting it to his own context.

15. The Stressful Revealing of the Christ (Mark 13:5–23, John 7:25–52, cf. Matt 23:37–39, 24:4–28)

Mark 13 speaks of a time of destruction, the destruction of Jerusalem and also of the world. Yet, negative though it is, this disintegrating process has other aspects: first, it leads to an effort to recognize the Christ (13:5–23), and then, it leads to the revelation of the Son of humanity (13:24–37).

John has taken this text and used it not of a distant cosmic disintegration but of the here-and-now disintegration which is involved in personal death—the initial, distant, sense of death which Jesus experiences in John 7 and the more immediate sense of death which he encounters in John 12 (esp. 12:20–50). Thus, the rewriting of Mark's eschatological chapter has been placed at the two extremes of the block which consists of John 7–12. In this way it lends a certain tone—the tone of the shadow of death—to the entire block.

The first part of the process of disintegration, the part which leads to efforts to recognize the Christ (Mark 13:5–23), is reflected in John 7:25–52—in the description of how, as the threat of death comes closer to Jesus, people try to recognize him as the Christ. (The later part, concerning the revelation of the Son of humanity, is reflected in 12:20–50).

Even though John's guiding text is Mark he makes use of the more elaborate version found in Matthew—so much so that it seems better, in Table 8.9, to refer to the text of Matthew.

This outline has obvious limitations. It does not make clear, for instance, why final birth pangs should be transformed into an obscure reference to death. And it does not take account of sources other than Matthew. (For instance, while the basic idea of preaching the gospel to the world seems to comes from Matthew, the precise image of Jesus' going to the Greeks appears to draw on Mark's account of Jesus going to the regions of Tyre and meeting the "Greek" woman, *Hellēnis*: Mark 7:24–30). Nor does the outline explain what seems to be an extraordinarily complex relationship between Matthew's great tribulation and John's last great day. Still it seems useful as a working hypothesis for further research.

Jesus is not harmed in John 7, any more than Jerusalem or the world come to an end in Matthew 24. Yet he lives in an atmosphere of foreboding—there are efforts to seize him; people are talking about his possible death; he knows he will die—and that foreboding is a personal microcosm of the larger dire predictions. Already in midlife, midway through the feast, there is an awareness of coming tribulation. He may be healthy and health-giving, yet even before death finally strikes, it will pass by at many times and in varied forms.

The process, however, is not altogether negative. In John, as in Matthew, the advance towards the end is marked by a hard-won awareness of the Christ, the anointed. It is as though the various dangers and sorrows can help to reveal a previously hidden dignity. One of the pitfalls however is to put one's trust in a dignity that is misplaced—to go after false Christs. Some of the people in John 7, for instance, connect Christhood with relationships: one should belong to a particular kind of family (Davidic descent) or a particular group of people (Beth-

Table 8.9.

Matthew 24:4–14: The Initial Sorrows	John 7:25–36: Midway through the Feast
Jerusalem killing the prophets (23:37–39).	Seeking to kill Jesus (7:25).
Beware of being misled concerning the Christ (24:4–5).	Actual confusion about the Christ (7:26–29).
Wars and rumors of wars—but the end is not yet (24:6)	They sought to seize him—but his hour had not yet come (7:30).
Further wars, famines, etc. (24:7).	A further effort to seize him (7:31–32).
The beginning of birth pangs (24:8)	The approach of departure (death) (7:33–34).
[Scandal, death (24:9–10).]	[Cf. 16:1–2 (Brown, 686)]
Many will be misled, and the gospel preached to the world (24:11–14).	Jews, not knowing the way, ask if Jesus will go to the Greeks (7:35–36).

Matthew 24:15–28: The Great Tribulation	John 7:37–52: The Last Great Day
Desolation in the holy place—following scripture, disruptive, yet for some bringing salvation (24:15–22).	Allusion to Jesus' death as involving an outflow/outburst, as following scripture, and as glory-giving (Details?) (7:37–39)
"Here is the Christ"—Do not believe it (24:23).	"This is the Christ"—division among them (Details?) (7:40–44).
There will be confusion about prophets (24:24–28).	Diverse opinions about Jesus (Details?) (7:45–52).

lehem); and there are certain places one should not come from (Galilee, 7:41–42). Jesus, however, places Christhood in another sphere—in a hidden relationship to the one who sent him (7:28), and it is this relationship which is to be increasingly revealed. Thus while Matthew, by referring to the various Christs, evokes the possibility of a positive development, John makes that possibility more explicit; he lays greater emphasis on the actual emergence and perception of the Christ. And he heightens the positive approach by setting the entire drama—dangers and all—in the context of a great feast. It is this latter idea—life as a fragile feast—which colors much of his transformation of Mark/Matthew.

16. The Revelation of the Son of Humanity (Mark 13:1–4, 24–37; John 12:20–50; cf. Matt 24:1–3, 29–44)

The first part of the eschatological text, concerning the revelation of the anointed (Mark 13:5–23; cf. Matt 24:4–28), has already been used by John—in the account of the sometimes ominous atmosphere at the feast of Tents (7:25–52). Now, as Jesus enters Jerusalem and death comes closer, he uses most of the remaining text: the account of the coming of the Son of humanity (Mark 13:1–4, 24–31; cf. Matt 24:1–3, 29–35) is a significant component in the account of how the coming of the Greeks heralds the glorification of the Son of humanity (John 12:20–36a). Table 8.10 gives a simplified outline.

In comparison with Mark, John is very different and very elaborate. Mark, for instance, says nothing about the dying of the grain of wheat and about its implications for discipleship (cf. John 12:24–26). Yet once Mark is seen as just one component, and once allowance is made for John's thorough rethinking of Mark's futuristic language, the relationship of the texts emerges as one of consistent dependence.

In place of Mark's picture of Jesus as foretelling the destruction of the Jewish temple (13:1–4), John depicts the coming of the Greeks (12:20–22). In other words, instead of foretelling the collapse of the old order, John intimates the down-to-earth emergence of the new. People will no longer admire a temple of stone (Mark); instead, as John suggests, they will seek to see a living person, Jesus.

And instead of speaking of the futuristic collapse of the universe—of the sun going dark and the stars falling (Mark 13:24–25)—John focuses on the human person and on the present death of the human person, physical death which destroys the body and the inner death which is a precondition of life.

The Mark/Matthew text, however frightening and obscure, is hopeful: it speaks of the Son of humanity as glorious (Mark 13:26–27; cf. Matt 24:30–31). In John the element of hope is clearer and closer: in

Table 8.10

Mark 13:1–4, 24–37	John 12:20–50
The destruction of the temple (13:1–4). Jesus and disciples leave temple. The time for looking at the stone temple is ending. Apart, four disciples question Jesus.	*The coming of the Greeks* (12:20–22). Greeks come to worship. The Greeks want to see Jesus. Two disciples come and tell Jesus.
The final cosmic collapse (13:24–25). In those days after the distress, the world will collapse.	*The final personal collapse* (12:23–26). The hour comes for glory, but it means dying.
And then—a sight of glory (13:26). They will see the Son of humanity coming in glory.	*Now? A prayer of glory* (12:27–28). Jesus, Son of humanity, is glorified in prayer.
Salvation for the chosen (13:27). Then the angels will gather the chosen from four winds.	*Salvation for all* (12:29–33). Jesus, if lifted up, will draw all to himself.
Know when the time is near (13:28–31). Observe the fig tree, and know when the Son of humanity is near. It will happen in this generation.	*The time is short* (12:34–36a). Who is the Son of humanity? for a little while the light is in you; walk in the light.
?	Unbelief (12:36b–43).
Watch for impending judgement (13:32–37). Cf. Matt 24:36–44: one will be taken, another will be left.	*Judgment is already delivered* (12:44–50). A variation on the idea of the two ways.

face of death, death even by crucifixion ("lifting up"), Jesus, through prayer, senses glory here and now. Mark already has a touch of universalism (". . . will gather . . . from the four winds"), but John is more explicit (". . . will draw all to myself").

The final parts of Mark 13—concerning the brevity of the time (13:28–31) and the need to watch for impending judgment (13:32–37)—have been so transformed in John that once more the emphasis falls not so much on the future as on the present. Though John follows Mark closely, he also draws on Matthew's interpretation of Mark, and this is particularly true in the final picture, concerning judgment (Mark 13:32–37, John 12:44–50; cf. Matt 24:36–44). It is Matthew, with the picture of two different fates ("one will be taken, one will be left") who provides an important building block for John's implied idea of the two ways.

The overall effect of John's radical transformation is to shift the focus of the eschatological discourse from an external and seemingly distant event to one which is much closer to home. The drama is not in the stars, but in ourselves.

17. The Meal, Including the Prospect of Judas's Betrayal and Peter's Denial (Mark 14:10–31, John 13)

Like Mark 11, Mark 14:1–42 is dominated by three distinct movements or scenes, but the sense of movement, instead of coming back three times to the Jerusalem temple, now progresses from one place to another—from the anointing at Bethany (14:1–9), to the meal in the upper room (14:10–26), to the prayer in Gethsemane (14:27–42). All three scenes evoke diverse aspects of Jesus' communion with people and God, but they are increasingly dominated by the specter of death. In the first two Jesus is reclining, in the third he is on the ground. All three begin with various references to one form or another of betrayal (by the authorities, 14:1–2; by Judas, 14:10–11; by Peter and the disciples, 14:27–31), and in varying ways the shadow of betrayal invades even the scenes of communion—the anointing is said to be a waste (14:4–5), someone at the meal will be a traitor (14:18–19), and those at the prayer fall asleep (14:34–41). Thus the sense of the encroaching end, so dramatically evoked in Mark 13, finds a complement in this picture of encroaching death.

In using this text, as shown in Table 8.11, John has broken it up and adapted it to his own distinct purposes.

Though the three main parts of Mark's text have been kept in the same order, they have not only been adapted; they have also been separated from each other. Thus their inherent connectedness is obscured. Yet John does not completely discard such connectedness. Rather, in his own way he preserves it. Thus the anointing in John may be separated from the meal, yet it has a basic aspect of continuity with it: it becomes an anointing of *feet*, and the meal involves a washing of feet. In other ways also the two are linked—by substantive issues such as the intimating of Jesus' death, and by details such as the references to

Table 8.11.

Mark 14:1–42	John
Anointing of head (including plot) (14:1–9).	Plot, anointing of feet (11:45–12:11).
The meal (including impending betrayal) (14:10–26).	The meal, washing of feet (chap. 13).
The final painful prayer (including foretelling of denial) (14:27–42).	The final ascentlike prayer (chap. 17).

"wiping" (Lindars, 416; the source for the image of anointing feet seems to have been Luke 7:38). And the prayer in John (chap. 17) may be separated from the meal (chap. 13), yet these two chapters (13 and 17) are so written that in various ways they balance and complement one another.

The essential factor is that in relocating the Markan accounts of the anointing, the meal, and the prayer, John has managed to preserve their affinity to one another.

This delicate blending—of freedom and fidelity—is found also in John's reworking of the second of these episodes, the meal (Mark 14:10–26). John uses the meal episode, but, in another move which preserves some of the connectedness of the three Markan texts, he combines it with part of the subsequent episode—with the denial passage which precedes the Gethsemane scene. Table 8.12 presents a simplified outline.

John has made major adaptations. In particular, the scene is no longer at passover (though it is passover-related). And the emphasis on the

Table 8.12.

Mark 14:10–31	John 13
Judas's impending betrayal (14:10–11).	
The meal, paschal and betrothallike, including the eucharist (14:12–26).	In the context of passover, a meal and Judas's impending betrayal, Jesus expresses love in washing feet (13:1–20).
Foretelling of denial (14:27–31).	Foretelling of betrayal and denial (13:21–38).

meal and eucharist (largely recast in John 6, esp. 6:52–58) has been replaced by the washing of the feet. John has used other sources and written a new account.

Yet there is continuity with Mark. John's inclusion, within the meal scene, of the news of Judas's impending betrayal, is in one sense an innovation (in Mark, the betrayal is mentioned *before* the meal). Yet, as is shown by Mark's careful structure—the division of 14:1–42 into the anointing (1–9), the meal (10–26), and the prayer (27–42)—the reference to betrayal is integral to the meal account. What John has done is to take that rather obscure connection and make it plain—by placing the betrayal reference clearly within the setting of the meal.

Likewise in reworking other elements. Mark seems to have obscure references to love and glory. The meal scene, which is introduced by the strange image of meeting a man carrying a pitcher of water (Mark 14:12–17), would seem, following Alter's method of analysis (1981, 52), to be a radical reshaping of the conventional betrothal scene. As such it indicates that the meal, which terminates in the eucharist, is an occasion of love. And it is with the idea of love that John's text begins (13:1). The difference, as so often, is that Mark is obscure, but John is clear; the idea of love is explicit.

Similarly with the idea of glory. In Mark the notion of glory is implied somewhat obscurely, particularly in the reference to drinking the fruit of the vine, new, in the realm of God (14:25). In John it is resoundingly explicit (13:31).

Thus in both Mark and John, but more clearly in John, the deadly process of treachery is set in the context of a greater phenomenon of love, love leading to glory.

18. *The Final Prayer (Mark 14:32–42, John 17)*

The difference between the texts could scarcely be clearer: in Mark's Gethsemane prayer Jesus is on the ground, struggling with the prospect of death; in John 17 his prayer is like an ascent to glory. John has used other sources and has composed another prayer.

Yet among John's sources, one consisted of the Markan scene, or rather of one aspect of the Markan scene. John never reproduces the dense Gethsemane scene in full. Rather he integrates aspects of it with other scenes, thus unpacking it as it were. In this manner he shows that the process of facing death, while it may indeed be concentrated in one episode, may also be spread out over a longer period—over several episodes.

Without attempting a full analysis, the Gethsemane scene, just after foretelling Peter's denial, shows at least three aspects of Jesus' reaction to death: deep distress and sadness (14:32–34); a dialogue with God in which, fallen to the ground, he passes from a wish for escape to initial acceptance (14:35–40); and a final phase in which, treating everything with serenity (sleeping disciples and the approaching traitor), he gives the order to rise (14:40–41). These three moments—distress, acceptance, and serenity—all have an equivalent in John, as shown in Table 8.13.

Apparently the two extremes of the Gethsemane prayer—distress and serenity—have been used by John near the two extremes of the last discourse. He has taken Mark's brief picture of serenity, of rising calmly to face death (14:41–42), and with the help of other sources, has expanded it into the ascentlike prayer. Even the idea of rising physically ("Rise, let us go") has been used at the two turning points of the last discourse—first at the end of chapter 14 ("Rise, let us go from here"), and again at the beginning of chapter 17, when Jesus lifts up his eyes.

19. The Narratives of Passion and Resurrection (Mark 14:43–16:8, John 18–21, cf. Matt 26:47– 28:20, Luke 20:66–24:53)

John's general affinity with the other gospels is at its clearest in the passion narratives. This does not prove that John depends on the others, but it means that the investigation of possible dependence is relatively easy—at least initially. The affinity with Mark is particularly strong, and once allowance is made for John's own contribution—for the purposefulness of the highly wrought theological dramas of sin (18:1–19:17a) and emerging glorification (19:17b–37)—the case for dependence is considerable.

The problem area is John's resurrection narrative; in several ways the fourth gospel is very different from the others. Yet, as Neirynck's study of the empty tomb stories has suggested (1984a, 161–87), the differences need not exclude a literary connection. There is, in fact, a basic continuity, one which, while using Mark as a starting point, draws especially on Matthew and Luke (see Table 8.14).

Among John's adaptations of these texts the most thorough are the

Table 8.13.

Mark	John
With Peter, James, and John he *becomes distressed and sad* (14:32–34).	Facing betrayal, just before foretelling Peter's denial, he *becomes deeply disturbed*. Peter and the beloved discuss it (13:21–24).
Fallen to the ground, he passes from a wish for escape ("that the hour might pass"), to acceptance (14:35–40).	When the hour comes, he moves quickly from the idea of escaping, to acceptance; and he speaks of the grain falling to the ground (12:23–28).
Apparent serenity: ". . . The hour is come . . . Rise, let us go . . ." (14:41–42).	*The ascentlike prayer*: "Father the hour has come . . ." (chap. 17).

Table 8.14.

Matthew 20	Luke 24	John 20–21
The empty tomb (20:1–10). (Cf. Mark 16:1–8).	The empty tomb (24:1–12). The recognition on the way to Emmaus (24:13–35). Appearance to disciples (joy, doubt, forgiveness, blessing God) (24: 36–53).	The empty tomb (20: 1–10). The recognition by Mary (20:11–18). Appearances to disciples (joy, forgiveness, doubt, God, blessing) (20:19–29).
Jewish misunderstanding of the resurrection (20:11–15). Galilee mountain: appearance and commissioning (20:16–20).		Galilee sea: appearance and commissioning (21:1–22). The brothers' misunderstanding of abiding (21:23).

elaboration of Matthew's brief Galilee scene into a considerable drama (John 21:1–22), and the reduction of the Jewish misunderstanding of the resurrection—a misunderstanding based on the false report of the bribed soldiers—to a brief mention of the brothers' misunderstanding of abiding (John 21:23).

The composing of John 21:1–22 involves a fusing of Matthew's scene with several other sources (see Appendix D, 169–70).

9

John's Systematic Use
of Matthew

An Outline
of Some Sections

One of the first general indications of John's knowledge of Matthew is not so much that both of them used Mark (though that in itself is important), but that the way in which Matthew did so—his absorbing and clarifying of Mark, and the fact that he added discourses—would seem to have provided a partial precedent for the work of John. In particular, Matthew's general way of arranging the discourses—each is preceded and introduced by narrative—furnishes an initial model for the procedure found in John.

In approaching the question of how John has actually adapted Matthew, it is useful to regard Matthew as consisting of four main elements. The references are simplified:

The infancy account: chapters 1–2.
Narratives: chapters 3–4, 8–9, 11–12, 14–17, 19–23.
Discourses: chapters 5–7, 10,   13,   18,   24–25.
The passion-and-resurrection account: chapters 26–28.

John's use of the infancy narrative is a puzzle, at least for the present writer. Perhaps its essence or part of its essence has been distilled into John 9. Apart from that, however, John's overall use of Matthew is reasonably clear. Matthew's narratives are drawn largely from Mark; and in absorbing Mark, John has also absorbed the corresponding Matthean texts, including apparently the Matthean elaborations. Thus, as already seen, John's trial scene (John 1:19–28), for instance, reflects not only the brief Markan account of Jesus' temptation but also the more elaborate account found in Matthew. Similarly with the passion-and-resurrection text: in incorporating Mark, John has also incorporated Matthew, including, for instance, Matthew's more extensive resurrection account.

With regard to Matthew's five discourses, one and a half of them (the parables, 13:1–52; and half the eschatological discourse, 24:1–44) are variations or elaborations of discourses already found in Mark, and as such, they belong—like the narratives—to the Markan framework. Thus the specifically Matthean discourses consist of just the remaining three and a half discourses—in broad terms, chaps. 5–7, 10, 18, and 24:45-chap. 25.

In summary form, the relationship of these texts to John is shown in Table 9.1.

The details, of course, are much more complex. Here, as in John's use of Mark, the orderly pattern seems, sometimes at least, to cover only one aspect of how Matthew has been used. Furthermore, even though Matthew's distinctive discourses provide something which could be called the center or foundation for several chapters of John, ultimately they are just one component, and besides they have been reworked radically in order to suit John's larger narrative. A closer idea of their relationship to the fourth gospel may be had from the outline in Table 9.2.

Table 9.1.

Matthew	John
The sermon on the Mount (4:23–chap. 7)	*The discourses in the temple* (chaps. 7–8).
The apostolic discourse (9:35–11:1).	*The discourses of the good shepherd* (chap. 10).
The discourse on the church (chap. 18).	*The last discourse* (chaps. 13–17).
Parables of departure, return and God-based *responsibility* (24:45–chap. 25).	

Table 9.2.

Matthew	John
A. Ascending the mountain to bring the law to completion (4:23–chap. 5) (cf. also Mark 7:1–23).	Going up to the temple and teaching the law truly (7:1–24).
Piety: externalism condemned (6:1–18; cf. 3:7–10, 23:13–36).	Jesus is in God's care (8:12–30).
God's care (6:18–34).	External believers condemned (8:31–59).
Blind judges, asking, fruitbearing, doing (7:1–12, 16–27).	? (Cf. chap. 9, 15:1–17).
The narrow gate; the sheeplike wolves; reactions (7:13–15, 28–29).	
B. Sheep, shepherd and workers (9:35–10:15).	Jesus as door/gate and shepherd; reactions (10:1–21).
Sheep among wolves; confess openly (10:16–11:1)	Jesus, surrounded by those who are not his sheep, speaks openly (10:22–42).
[10:17b–25, hated by all].	[Cf. John 15:18–16:4a].
C. Becoming little, etc.; forgiveness (chap. 18).	Self-emptying, etc. (chaps. 13–17) (on forgiveness, cf. 20:19–23, 21:21–35).
The sense of God which leads to down-to-earth responsibility (24:45–chap. 25).	The washing of the feet (13:1–20).

Section A: The Sermon on the Mount and the Discourse in the Temple (Matt 4:23–chap. 7, John 7–8)

The thoroughness of John's reworking of Matthew's discourses may be seen immediately in the way he has transformed the Sermon on the Mount and integrated it with other material. This brief analysis concentrates on just some limited aspects of that transformation, particularly on the way in which 4:23–chap. 7 (or most of it) has been integrated with later sections of Matthew (with most of 23:13–24:28) and with some of Mark (including some of the Mark/Matthew eschatological discourse). The relationship of the texts is summarized in Table 9.3.

John makes no clear reference either to the Sermon on the Mount or to the later discourses recorded in Matthew (Matt 23:13–24:28). In-

Table 9.3.

Matt 4:23–chap. 6 (plus most of 23:13–24:28)	John 7–8
1. *Jesus goes about in Galilee* (4:23–25). (Mark 11:12–14, 20–25: the withered fig tree, and faith . . .). *Went up to the mountain* and taught (5:1–2).	*Jesus walks, stays in Galilee* (7:1–9). The brothers' [=Jews] deathly faithlessness (7:3–8). *Went up to the temple* and taught (7:10–14).
2. The Beatitudes (5:3–12). Salt, *light* of the world (5:13–16). The antitheses: the law is deepened and oriented to God. (5:17–48). [Mark 7:1–23: Jesus condemns the godless approach to Moses.]	? Jesus teaches the law in a discerning God-centered way (7:15–24).
3. Jesus condemns *externalism* (23:13–36). *The impending fall of Jerusalem* and the revealing of the Christ (in symbolic futuristic language) (23:37–39, 24:4–28; cf. Mark 13:5–23)	*The impending death of Jesus* and the revealing of him as the Christ (in language that is more plain and present) (7:25–52).
4. Alms, prayer, fasting: against *externalism* (6:1–18).	Jesus, *light* of the world, is in *God's care* (8:12–30).
5. *God's care* (6:19–34).	Jesus condemns *externalism* among Jewish believers (8:31–59). See esp. John 10:1–21, 15:1–17.
6. Blind judgment, prayer, the gate to life, sheeplike wolves, the two ways (chap. 7).	

stead, the discourses, which he has placed near the center of his gospel (chaps. 7–8), are such that in various ways they reflect and combine significant sections of both Matthean texts. (It is as though John regarded the Matthean texts as inherently connected.) The result— delivered in the temple at the feast of Tents—is a text which retains little either of the visionary idealism of Matthew 5–7 or of the dread apocalypticism of Matthew 23–25. Instead it gives a filtered application of these diverse visions, a sense of how they impinge on the life of Jesus and those around him. Thus while Jesus does not ascend a mountain to deliver a Moses-like declaration on the law, he does ascend to the Jerusalem temple, and there, in the context of specific cases, he implies that the administration of the law requires a new mode of understanding. And Jesus does not speak of the end of Jerusalem or of the world, but he does evoke death, the end of life itself. (The central image of the feast, that of a tent, evokes the fragility of life; the body is like a tent; see Isa 38:12, 2 Cor 5:1–5.) It is with the threat of Jesus' death that the feast is introduced (7:1–2), and an allusion to his death likewise marks the feast's high point, its "last day" (7:37–39). Thus the concept of the last day begins to move from a distant, general, future to the concrete human experience, felt even in life, of facing death.

1. Going about Galilee, and Then Going up and Teaching (Matt 4:23–5:2, John 7:1–14)

Matthew tells of Jesus going around Galilee, receiving a positive response, and then of his ascending the mountain to teach. John's description is somewhat similar (Jesus walks around Galilee and then ascends to the Jerusalem temple to teach); but there is one central difference— the response, delivered by his brothers, is extremely negative. Where Matthew has receptiveness and healing, John has disbelief and a counsel of death. In other words, he follows Matthew's framework, but not his central ingredient. The framework comes from the time of the initial, positive, reaction to Jesus, but the central ingredient represents a later development.

It is not clear whence John drew the negative picture of the disbelieving brothers—in some ways their failed vitality is like the failed vitality of the fig tree (Mark 11:12–14, 20–25; both the brothers and the withered tree represent the inner withering of the Jews)—but, whatever its origin, the picture of disbelief suits the requirements of John's text: it conforms to the fact that while the beginning of the gospel was generally positive, the time has come, especially in chapters 7 and 8, to begin facing the presence of darkness.

2. Teaching the Law in a Discerning God-Centered Way (Matt 5:17–48, John 7:15–24, cf. Mark 7:1–23)

Matthew 5 consists essentially of three passages—the Beatitudes (5:3–12), the sayings on salt and light (5:13–16), and the antitheses (5:17–48). It is not clear (at least not to the present writer) what John has done with the Beatitudes. As for the sayings on salt and light, they seem to have been synthesized and transmuted so as to help form Jesus' declaration, "I am the light of the world . . ." (John 8:12)—a variation on the Johannine technique of turning something parabolic or parablelike into an "I am . . ." saying.

It is the influence of the antitheses which is most tangible in John 7–8. In their picture of Jesus as deepening the law—breaking through its letter so as to find a greater spirit—they provide the basis for John's picture of Jesus' initial teaching in the temple (7:15–24). In place of the several statements and counterstatements, John gives one basic, synthesized, contrast: you use the law to cut, but I use it to make a person whole (7:22–23).

But while Matthew thus supplies a certain basis or framework, John's text contains several other elements, and for these the best source appears to be Mark's account (7:1–23) of how Jesus condemns the superficial interpretation of the law. As already seen in the preceding chapter, both texts (Mark 7:1–23; John 7:15–24) contain a series of related factors: first, the idea that true teaching comes not from human tradition or effort but from God (Mark 7:1–8, John 7:15–18); secondly, that Jewish teaching destroys what comes from God (Mark 7:9–13, it nullifies God's word; John 7:19–20, the Jews seek to kill Jesus); and thirdly, that the prevailing teaching is superficial and thus fails to understand what is within, what is internal (Mark 7:14–23, John 7:24).

John's fundamental procedure, in dealing with both texts (Matt 5:17–48, Mark 7:1–23), is one of dense synthesis. He has taken both the positive program of Matthew and the severe condemnations of Mark and has reduced them drastically but accurately into a new form.

3. Externalism and Impending Collapse
(Matt 23:13–39, 24:4–28, [cf. Mark 13:5–23];
John 7:25–52)

As already indicated in dealing with Mark, the picture of impending collapse and of the effort to recognize the Christ (Mark 13:5–23, Matt 24:4–28) does indeed come first from Mark, yet John's use of it (in 7:25–52) relies especially on Matthew. In thus using part of Matthew 24 (including the end of Matthew 23 [37–39]), John has gone further: he has drawn on the earlier part of chapter 23 (13–36)—a text which suits his next topic, externalism.

4. Jesus Condemns Externalism (Matt 6:1–18, 23:13–36, [cf. 3:7–10]; John 8:31–59)

The Matthean discourses contain two major passages in which Jesus condemns externalism—the address on positive piety (on alms, on prayer, including the Our Father, and on fasting, 6:1–18) and the indictment of the scribes and Pharisees, the litany of woes (23:13–36). Nowhere else in the NT, save in these two passages, does one find repeated use of the word "hypocrite."

Closely associated with the indictments is the similar indictment which was issued by John the Baptist—a warning not to rely on physical descent from Abraham (Matt 3:7–9).

It is probably because of their inherent connectedness that John has combined these texts. In diverse ways he has used them as components for the harsh attack on superficial Jewish believers (8:31–59). Of course, he may also have used some parts of them for other purposes—in particular the Our Father (Matt 6:9–13) as a component of chapter 17. But their primary use has been in 8:31–59.

John's dependence on the address concerning piety (Matt 6:1–18) is limited but important. The essence of the address is the need to move beyond externalism, beyond limiting oneself to the interaction between one's outer self and other people, an interaction which often consists of putting on a show. In place of such theatrics it opens up the possibility of being deeply grounded in God, in "your Father," the one who sees in secret. For Matthew, therefore, the alternatives are relatively simple: externalism versus groundedness in God.

John takes this idea and develops it further. He not only speaks of groundedness in God—something which is found supremely in Jesus (cf. John 8:12–30). He then goes on to show that the alternative is more than mere externalism; it is something deeper, groundedness of another kind—in the devil (8:44). As Matthew had repeated the phrase "your Father" (*patēr hymōn*, plural, 6:1, 8, 14, 15) so John also repeats it (8:41, 42, 44, 56, and perhaps 8:38), but apart from the final instance (8:56), it is with regard to the devil that John uses it. Such frequent repetition, in both texts, is significant; it is a phenomenon which does not otherwise occur in the NT, and thus it confirms the connectedness of the texts. John has used Matthew but has sharpened the alternative: no longer groundedness in God versus externalism, but groundedness in God versus groundedness in the devil. It is a sharpening which brings an edge of dualism.

John's dependence on the litany of woes (Matt 23:13–36) helps to account for the dualistic edge. In these texts it is implied that the scribes and Pharisees are both sons of hell and sons of murderers—from the murder of Abel onwards (23:15, 31, 35). Thus the way is prepared for John's synthesizing statement that the superficial Jewish believers are children of the devil, the one who was a murderer from the beginning (John 8:44).

John's dependence on the Baptist's initial indictment (Matt 3:7–9) is also important. It is from this preliminary condemnation that John draws his first accusation against the Jews—their reliance on descent, on the physical fatherhood of Abraham (John 8:33, 37, 39–40)—and it is within the framework of this false reliance on physical fatherhood that he proceeds to uncover a further, lethal, fatherhood.

Thus when taken together the three Matthean texts (3:7–9, 6:1–18, 23:13–36) provide important aspects both of John's framework and of his most searing accusation. First, Matt 3:7–9 gives the empty, outward, fatherhood. Then, Matt 6:1–18 supplies the idea of a fatherhood which is internal and positive. And finally Matt 23:13–36 provides part of the concept of a fatherhood which is internal and negative.

John's procedure once again is primarily one of synthesis. Matthean passages, which are inherently connected, have been assembled and rewritten. And John has also made a major adaptation: the accusation of externalism is no longer directed at Jewish leaders but at Jewish believers—a reference apparently to the fact that the superficiality which had once been associated with the Pharisees has now gained entry among Jesus' own followers.

5. God's Care Even Amid Dangers (Matt 6:19–34, John 8:12–30)

Matthew 6:19–34 is a call to focus increasingly on God, even amid all the distractions and worries of life. The first part of the text (6:19–24) centers around the ideas of treasure, light and single-minded service, and it suggests that God be the one to whom one entrusts oneself.

The second part (6:25–34), while continuing to speak of human trust, focuses more explicitly on God ("your heavenly Father . . . God . . . your heavenly Father") and, by referring to God's care for the birds of the sky and the lilies of the field, it seeks to draw the worrisome human into the surpassing world of God's presence.

It would appear that John has used these texts as one component of his description of Jesus' reliance on God (8:12–30). The similarities between the texts are slender, and if it were not for the context—the fact that John has used other sections of Matthew—it is doubtful if these passages could be seen as connected. Table 9.4 shows a simplified outline. In speaking of Jesus as the light of the world, John has apparently combined two Matthean texts—"You are the light . . ." (cf. 5:13–16), and "The light of the body . . ." (6:22–23).

One of the most fundamental changes wrought by John is that, as in many other cases, he has gone from the general to the specific. He has taken the broad exhortations of the Sermon on the Mount and shown them in action, as it were—in the actual life of Jesus. Thus the idea of seeking the surpassing God is illustrated and intensified in the picture of Jesus who, even in face of the greatest anxiety, that of death, speaks in the language of God: "the beginning (*archēn*) . . . I am" (John 8:25, 28).

6. Blind Judges, Prayer, the Narrow Gate, etc. (Matthew 7; cf. John 10, 15)

Apparently John has divided Matthew 7 into various parts and used these parts at different points throughout his gospel. Without attempting to trace the details of his procedure, two points may be noted. The emphasis on prayer and fruit bearing (Matt 7:7–11, 15–20) has considerable affinity with part of the parable of the vine (John 15:1–17); and, more clearly, the mention of the narrow gate, the sheeplike wolves, and the people's reaction (Matt 7:13–15, 28–29) has affinity with the parable of good shepherd (and, to some degree, with the reaction to it: John 10:1–21).

Table 9.4.

Matt 6:19–34	John 8:12–30
Treasure in heaven. The light of the body. Serve one master (6:19–24).	Jesus, light of the world, in deep union with God, speaks in the treasury (8:12–20).
Amid anxieties seek the surpassing God (6:25–34).	In face of death, Jesus is completely one with God (8:21–30).

Section B: The Apostolic Discourse and the Discourses by the Good Shepherd (Matt 9:35–11:1, John 10)

In simplified terms the apostolic discourse consists of two sections—the (initial) commissioning (9:35–10:15) and the (ensuing) conflict (10:16–11:1). The commissioning tells of the circumstances which led to the calling of the twelve disciples and also of the quality of the work which they were to carry out. The entire text is a unity; the disciples' work is a precise continuation of that of Jesus (cf. 9:35, 10:1), and to a significant extent the text as a whole is governed by a single image—that of a shepherd caring for sheep (cf. 9:36, 10:6).

The second section, the conflict (10:16–11:1), tells of the acute difficulties through which the disciples will have to pass—hatred, dangers, death. Yet through all this "the Father" is with them. The opening image in this section, the image which to some extent holds it together, is that of sheep among wolves (10:16).

This twofold division has been used by John as a partial framework for chapter 10. Table 9.5 presents a simplified outline.

The most basic aspect of this adaptation is that Matthew's description of a whole mission has been concentrated into an image of Jesus: "I am the good shepherd. . . ." This is a further variation on the Johannine technique of rendering some parable or picture of the divine realm into an "I am . . ." discourse. The action has been moved into Jesus as it were. But the disciples and the mission are not forgotten. John's picture of Jesus is so developed that in various ways it contains the idea of disciples and mission: the shepherd dies for the disciples (John 10:11); and it is he, above all, who is on a mission (" . . . sent into the world," 10:36). Thus Matthew's essential idea, that of a self-less shepherdlike

Table 9.5.

Matthew	John
The compassionate shepherd sends out workers (9:35–10:15).	The good shepherd (10:1–21).
Sent out as sheep in the midst of wolves (10:16–11:1).	Jesus is surrounded by those who are not his sheep (10:22–42).

mission, has been retained, but the focus has shifted from the outward mission to the mission's ultimate roots—to the self-giving of God as manifested in Jesus.

Yet John does not become lost in remote beginnings. It is he, even more than Matthew, who gives a picture of an actual mission in action. Instead of the several general images of danger—the sheep in the midst of wolves (Matt 10:16–42)—John shows Jesus as being in actual danger, as being surrounded by people who want to stone him (John 10:22–39). Thus John seeks to fill out the extent and meaning of mission—from its roots in God's love to the need to face an angry crowd.

The details of John's procedure are summarized in Table 9.6.

It is in Matthew 7 also that one finds, in rapid succession, the images of the gate (*pylē*) and the sheep (7:13–15). John apparently took these elements from the final stages of the Sermon on the Mount and combined them with the later sheep-and-shepherd imagery (Matt 9:36, 10:6)

Table 9.6.

Matthew chap. 7, 9:35–11:1	John 10
Blind judges (7:1–6) (cf. 23:16, 19, 26).	Cf. John 9?
Asking, fruitbearing, doing (7:7–12, 16–27).	Cf. John 15:1–17?
The narrow gate to life (7:13–14). Beware of sheeplike wolves (7:15). Reaction (7:28–29).	
Sheep, shepherd and workers (9:35–10:15).	*Jesus as door/gate and shepherd* (10:1–18). Reactions (10:19–21).
Sheep among wolves (10:16–17a, 26–31).	*Jesus surrounded* by those who are not his sheep (10:22–30).
Hated by all (10:17b–25).	Cf 15:18–16:4a.
Confession, conflict, union (10:32–42).	*Revelation, stoning, union* (10:31–42).
Confession, linking one to the Father (10:32–33).	Jesus' works reflect the Father (10:32).
Conflict: sword and cross (10:34–39).	Stoning (10:31, 33).
Identification of one sent with the Sender (10:40–42).	Jesus, sent into the world is in the sending Father (10:34, 38).
Conclusion and *departure* (11:1).	*Departure* and reaction (10:40–42).

to help produce the text concerning the *thyra*, "door/gate," and the shepherd (John 10:1–19). Furthermore, the reaction to the sermon (Matt 7:28–29) has been used as one element in composing the reaction accounts in John 10.

John, of course, has wrought a major transformation. The details of the first gospel have been omitted or distilled and the parable of the good shepherd has been subjected to the rigorous requirement of falling into line with the rest of the fourth gospel, particularly with the closely coordinated series of descent-ascent texts.

As regards the second section of the apostolic discourse, concerning conflict (Matt 10:16–11:1), it is generally agreed that some of it (10:17b–25) has a clear affinity with the later picture of the world's hatred for the disciples (John 15:18–16:4a; for details, see Brown, 694). This affinity, however, is but part of a larger, more complex phenomenon: the conflict is reflected not only in the future fates of the disciples, but also in the present fate of Jesus—in the hostility of the Jews as they surround him in Solomon's portico in winter (John 10:22–39). However, the affinity of Matthew 10 with John 10 is not at all as clear as the affinity of Matthew 10 with John 15:18–16:4a. The context of John 10 demands a more radical transformation, and the relationship of the texts is correspondingly more intricate. This relationship may be summarized under the two following headings.

In the Midst of Danger, Yet Speaking Openly
(Matt 10:16–17a, 26–31; John 10:22–30)

The image of the disciples as being in the midst of wolves has been converted into the image of Jesus as being surrounded by the Jews. The texts share several elements:

> The sense of facing some kind of trial or questioning (Matt 10:17a, John 10:23–24a).
> Even in danger, speaking plainly (Matt 10:26–27, John 10:24–25).
> The image of darkness or winter (Matt 10:27, John 10:22).
> Not fearing those who may kill/stone (Matt 10:28a, John 10:31).
> The importance of life which lasts (Matt 10:28b, John 10:28a).
> God's watchful care for the disciples/Jesus (Matt 10:29–31, John 10:28b–30).

*Revealing the Loving God, and Taking the
Consequences Both of Conflict and Union
(Matt 10:32–42, John 10:31–42)*

Both texts speak of an outward process, which implies an inner relationship with the loving God, the Father. Confessing Jesus before people links one to the Father and thus reflects the Father (Matt 10:32–33). And Jesus' revealing of good works to the Jews likewise reflects the Father (John 10:32). The essence of both texts therefore is that one's external life is grounded on an internal foundation.

But the living of such a life—a life which is not superficial—causes conflict; the internal relationship often goes against the grain and so people resist it. Matthew (10:34–39), therefore, speaks of Jesus as bringing a sword, as dividing people, and so one must bear pain—the cross. John (10:31, 33) shows Jesus as having to face stoning.

Yet this conflict is worth enduring. More clearly than before both texts now return to the idea which previously had simply been implied—that of union between the one sent and the Sender. Matthew states the principle in three different ways (10:40–42): "Whoever receives you. . . . Whoever receives a prophet. . . . Whoever gives a drink. . . ."), and as well as speaking of (implied) union, refers also to reward (" . . . shall receive reward . . . shall not lose their reward . . ."). John does not refer either to the future or to "reward." Instead he synthesizes these various elements into something simpler, clearer, and more present—here-and-now union with God: ". . . the Father is in me and I am in the Father" (John 10:34–38).

At the end, Jesus departs: he goes away from there in order to teach in their towns (Matt 11:1); and he goes across the Jordan (John 10:40–42). Matthew's text apparently has supplied just one small component to John's more elaborate picture.

Section C: Matthew: the Discourse on the Church (chap. 18) and the Parables of Departure, Return, and God-based Responsibility (24:45–chap. 25); John: the Last Discourse (chaps. 13–17)

John's procedure of synthesizing reaches a new level of complexity in the last discourse (chaps. 13–17) and in the final chapter (chap. 21).

This increasing complexity is understandable—it corresponds to the way in which these concluding texts draw things together—but it makes the tracing of sources considerably more difficult. And the sheer volume of the last discourse makes the difficulty all the greater. Consequently John's use at this point of certain aspects of Matthew 18 and Matt 24:45-chap. 25 constitutes just one element of a much more intricate picture.

John's apparent use of Matthew 18 may be dealt with briefly. The initial idea—that within God's realm those disciples who humble themselves in order to become like children are the greatest (Matt 18:1–5)—has significant links with John 13, a chapter in which the one who is greatest humbles himself and addresses the disciples as children (cf. John 13:1–5, 16, 33). The next text—which on the one hand speaks of the need to cut off whatever impedes the development of the "child" ("little one") and on the other pronounces woe on the world because it so impedes people ("scandalizes," Matt 18:6–9)—has been used apparently in John 15:1–16:4a, first to contribute to the idea that development involves pruning (15:1–17, esp. vv 2–6), and then to help describe the sense of distance between the developing disciple and the scandalous world (15:18–16:4a). The third passage—concerning the "child" whose angel looks on the face of God in heaven and whom the shepherdlike God does not want to lose (Matt 18:10–14)—would seem to be reflected in the Jesus who raises his eyes to heaven and who speaks, among other things, of his care that none be lost (John 17, esp. 17:1a, 12). Thus the varying images of the greatest, childlike, disciple correspond broadly to the three stages of discipleship in John 13–17.

The later part of Matthew 18, concerning sin and forgiveness (15–35) would seem to have been used at the end of John's gospel, first in the granting of power to forgive sin (John 20:19–23; cf. Matt 18:15–20) and then perhaps in the picture of the rehabilitation of Peter (John 21:9, 15–23; cf. Matt 18:21–35).

The other text, Matt 24:45–chap. 25, is not only the conclusion of the eschatological discourse; as a block it is also distinctly Matthean. It is colorful and largely parabolic, dealing in effect with Jesus' departure and return, and, above all, dealing with the disciples' responsibility in the interim, including their responsibility for one another:

24:45–51: The Lord appoints a servant until he returns.
25:1–13:   The bridesmaids are to await the coming of the groom.
25:14–30: The departing Lord gives talents, and later returns.

25:31–46: The Lord comes and judges the world on the basis of kindness.

A glance at these four texts shows their fundamental kinship with the last discourse. The theme of departure and return, so central and explicit in John 13–17, is found already within these passages in varying forms and with varying degrees of explicitness. So also is the theme of responsibility. The beginning of the first parable, for instance, concerning the true servant whom the Lord appoints to take care of the household (Matt 24:45–51, esp. vv 45–47), is closely echoed in Jesus' message, delivered in the context of the footwashing, that the disciples should be like servants (John 13:15–17).

This need not mean that John's dependence on Matt 24:45–chapter 25 is limited to chapters 13 to 17; rather, as in the case of Matthew 18, certain sections or aspects of 24:45–chapter 25 may have been used in building other chapters of John. But the basic affinity is strong.

It is within this context that the question arises as to the sources of the actual footwashing account. Matthew makes no mention of washing feet. Yet Matthew is not irrelevant. In the climactic account of the judgment of all people (Matt 25:31–46) the decisive criterion is that of down-to-earth human kindness—attending to the hungry, the thirsty, the stranger, the naked, the sick, and the imprisoned. And it is precisely that idea which is reflected—reflected with increased simplicity, vividness, and power—in the picture of washing feet.

There are a number of elements which connect the two texts. In both cases it is not easy to understand how the divine can be involved in something so human and humble. In Matthew's scene people ask when it was that they saw the Lord hungry and thirsty. And Peter asks how the Lord can wash the feet of his disciple. In other words, it is hard to see that God is involved in something so menial. But eventually it can be grasped. The people understand it at the judgment, and Peter "will understand it later." It is by respecting this humble divine presence that one achieves a lasting place or share with God (Matt 25:46, John 13:8); it is by such kindness that discipleship is judged (cf. John 13:35).

Thus the multifaceted image which climaxes Matthew's discourses appears to have contributed to the single image which most governs John's last discourse.

10

John's Systematic Use
of Part of Luke-Acts

Brown (330, 184) notes that the character of Nicodemus (John 3:1–21) is like that of Gamaliel (Acts 5:34–39), and that the account of Samaria's acceptance of Jesus (John 4:1–42) would seem to reflect the evangelization of Samaria by Philip, Peter, and John—an event which is reported in Acts 8:1b–25. Brown does not suggest that the texts are connected—that John used Acts—but it is on the basis of the texts that he makes his observations, and so there is obviously some form of link, literary or otherwise, between the texts. An investigation of the adjacent episodes in Table 10.1 shows further connectedness.

The text of Acts alone does not account fully for John. In itself it is insufficient, and besides, it has already been seen that to some degree John's text is based on Mark and Matthew. What Acts supplies therefore is a complementary component.

Bearing Witness to the Jews and to the Open-minded Pharisee (Gamaliel/Nicodemus) (Acts 5:17–42, John 3:1–21)

In Acts the hostility of the Jewish authorities leads first to a drama of light and darkness—the apostles are released at night by an angel but the authorities are left "in the dark" (5:17–26)—and then to a Sanhedrin scene in which the apostles bear witness concerning the saving role of Jesus. The apostles would have been put to death, but Gamaliel intervened, aware that this new movement might be from God.

In John 3:1–21 Nicodemus comes by night, shows an awareness that

Table 10.1.

Acts	John
Gamaliel (5:17–42), a Pharisee, a member of the Sanhedrin.	*Nicodemus* (3:1–21), a Pharisee, a ruler of the Jews.
Stephen (6:1–8:1a), martyr, sees the heavens opened.	*John* (3:22–36), the fading bearer of *martyria,* speaks of one coming from heaven.
Samaria (8:1b–25), accepts evangelization, and the Spirit.	*The Samaritan woman* (4:1–42), asks for living water, and evangelizes the city.
The Ethiopian eunuch (8:26–40), a royal official, believes the word about Jesus.	*The man from Capernaum* (4:43–54), a royal official believes Jesus' word.

Jesus is from God, and then becomes involved in a discussion in which the voice of Jesus becomes like that of the Christian community addressing the Jews (3:11: "we witness what we have seen, and you do not receive our witness"). Thus the similarity between the characters of Nicodemus and Gamaliel is part of a much larger similarity between two whole dramas.

In Tension with the Administrators of the Old Order, the Witness-bearer Who Truly Represents It (Stephen/John) Sees the One Who Is from Heaven (Acts 6:1–8:1a, John 3:22–36)

Stephen is described at length (Acts 6) both as being a powerful positive witness and as being in tension with the old order (with both synagogue and Sanhedrin). His speech (7:1–53) confirms that role: he speaks like an angel who has understood the essence of the old order, but his understanding and his witness bring him into tension with those who administer it. Then, as he faces death (7:54–8:1a), he leaves behind his preoccupation with the old order, and seeing heaven open, commits himself, even while sinking to his knees, to the glorious Jesus who is to receive him.

The portrait of John the baptizer as given in the fourth gospel (3:22–

36) is much more compact but is essentially similar to that of Stephen. John is first represented as being both a witness who in some way represents the old preparatory order and as being in tension with the Jew(s) (3:22–30). Then, after his demise has been evoked (cf. 3:24, 30), he speaks of the one who comes from heaven (3:31–36).

Though the Stephen text is extensive, it is not the only source used in John 3:22–36. As noted earlier, the image of the bridegroom (John 3:29) seems to come, in large part, from a related episode in Mark (2:18–22, concerning fasting). Thus, brief though John's text may be, it involves a dense synthesizing of diverse components.

The Evangelization of Samaria (Acts 8:1b–25, John 4:1–42)

As seen already, the account of the woman of Samaria seems to synthesize a significant part of several major Markan episodes (5:1–20, 25–34; 6:1–29). Yet important aspects of John's text remain unaccounted for—among them the picture of the large-scale conversion of the city of Samaria. It is this element which is supplied by Acts. An outline is presented in Table 10.2.

Apart from Acts 1:8 and 9:31, these are the only NT texts which refer in rapid succession to "Judea" and "Samaria." The unbroken phrase "gift of God" (*dōrea tou theou*: Acts 8:20, John 4:10) does not otherwise occur in the NT. Brown (184) emphasizes the shared idea of two levels of workers: the distinction between the original evangelizer Philip (Acts 8:9–13) and the subsequent Spirit-filled work of Peter and John (Acts 8:14–17) is roughly equivalent to John's distinction between sowers and reapers (John 4:37–38). John has distilled the essence of the account in Acts and with light touches has integrated it with other material.

The Royal Official (from Ethiopia/Capernaum) (Acts 8:26–40, John 4:43–54)

In this instance it is particularly clear that John is not relying on Acts alone. The picture of the royal official from Capernaum, whose son was dying, is indebted partly to Mark's account of Jairus and his sick daughter (Mark 5:21–24, 35–43) and even more so to Matthew's report concerning the Capernaum centurion whose servant was sick (Matt 8:5–13; cf. Luke 7:1–10). But Acts has also been used, at least in a minor

Table 10.2.

Acts	John
Movement from Jerusalem to Judea and Samaria (8:1b–3).	Movement (begun in Jerusalem) from Judea through Samaria (4:1–6).
Philip goes to the city and preaches Christ; people accept (8:4–8).	The woman, thinking physically, misunderstands "the gift of God" (4:7–15).
Two levels of believing, without and with the Spirit (8:13–17). (Two levels of workers.)	Two levels of worship, without and with the spirit (4:16–26).
Simon, thinking of money, misunderstands "the gift of God" (8:18–24).	The woman goes to the city and preaches Christ; many believe (4:28–39). (Discussion regarding two levels of workers.)

way. It is Acts, with its reference to the eunuch as the treasurer of the Ethiopian queen (*basilissa*, 8:27) which supplies the leading idea of someone who is a royal official (*basilikos*, 4:46,49; the word *basilikos*, otherwise virtually unknown in the NT, is found twice in Acts 12). It is Acts also with its several references to water (8:36–39) which helps, to some degree, to fill in another leading aspect of John's text—the opening reference to the water which was made wine (John 4:46). And, in a more general way, concerning John's report that the official and his *whole household believed* (4:53), "the best parallels are found in Acts" (Brown, 196; cf. Acts 10:2; 11:14; 16:15, 31, 34; 18:8). Thus while John's use of Acts 8:26–40 may not be extensive, it is not to be dismissed.

Conclusion

John's indebtedness to Luke-Acts varies greatly from episode to episode. Concerning Nicodemus, for instance, it is central, but concerning the royal official it seems to be slight.

Yet, while allowing for variations, it is consistent. All four characters who come to Jesus in chapters 3 and 4, or who speak of him, are so described that they reflect, systematically, the leading episodes and characters of Acts 5:17–chap. 8.

Furthermore, it would appear that this systematic dependence on Luke-Acts continues through the whole of John's gospel. However, rather than attempt to analyze that dependence, even in the brief way that has been done for chapters 3 and 4, it seems better simply to provide, in an appendix, a skeletal outline which may be useful in further research. (See Appendix D.)

11

John's Systematic Use of the Pentateuch

Thus far much of John 4:1–42 has been accounted for by invoking John's use of Mark (5:1–24, 35–43; 6:1–29) and Acts (8:1b–25); but not all of John 4:1–42 has been accounted for, particularly its quality of personal encounter. There are indeed instances of personal meeting in the Markan texts and in Acts 8:1b–25, but none of these passages contains the flavor of a prolonged personal discussion, such as occurs between Jesus and the woman at the well. To find this factor one must look at another of John's sources—the Pentateuch.

Within the Pentateuch there are two literary conventions which place particular emphasis on personal encounter—the betrothal scene, which generally takes place at a well (as in Gen 24, 29:1–30; Exod 2:11–22), and the prophetic vision (particularly as in Exod 2:23–chap. 4; cf. esp. Isa 6, Jer 1). In the first the encounter is with a woman, and in the second with God.

In the Genesis texts (chaps. 24 and 29) the betrothal scenes are quite elaborate, but not so in the case of Moses. For Moses the two encounters come together (at least within the text)—first with his future wife (Exod 2:11–22), then with God (Exod 2:23–chap. 4)—and in the apparent tension between the two, the betrothal scene loses. It is reduced to a brief account, scarcely recognizable as a betrothal scene, and is quite overshadowed by the dramatic mountain scene of the burning bush and by the enigmatic revelation of the "I am." The relationship between the two scenes is telling: it is God rather than the woman who shall be at the center of Moses' life.

Jesus' discussion with the Samaritan woman reflects both scenes. The first part of the discussion (John 4:7–15) centers around the well and water. In the second part (4:16–26), which has no reference to a well or water, attention suddenly focuses on the previously-unmentioned mountain (4:20–21), on the emergence of Jesus as a prophet (4:19), and finally on Jesus' "I am . . ." (4:26).

But while John has thus preserved the essence of both scenes, he has worked a major change. Instead of down-playing the betrothal scene to the benefit of the prophetic call, he has blended the two and has done so in such a way that, while the prophetic encounter is respected, it is integrated into the larger context of a betrothal scene, which has been transformed and, in a sense, spiritualized. In other words, the apparent tension between the two OT scenes, between the physical and the spiritual, has, in a certain sense, been resolved: the more physical scene, the betrothal, has been spiritualized and has thus been made capable of absorbing the other, spiritual, scene.

This does not mean that John has taken leave of the physical. The entire combination of experiences, both of betrothal and of prophetic call, are centered around the most down-to-earth of characters, the woman of Samaria. It is she, amid her daily work, who begins to become aware of a life-giving presence such as she had not known before. And though it is Jesus who is first recognized as a prophet, it is to the woman ultimately that the prophetic call is focused: there at the mountain she receives the revelation, and it is she who then goes and announces it to the city. Moses of old had come back from the mountain with a message of freedom. Now she also comes, announcing freedom of another kind. The sense of a long and rather personal discussion—a discussion which in the course of Moses' call sometimes tends to become sidetracked—finds in her case an expression which is clearly focused, close to the bone.

A Closer Analysis

The details of John's use of the beginning of Exodus seem to be quite complex and extend beyond the texts just discussed. See Table 11.1.

From a Situation of (Apparent) Hostility to a Foreign Land and a Well (Exod 1:1–2:15, John 4:1–6)

Against the background of Israel's increasing numbers, Exodus begins by telling of oppression and of the saving of the condemned boys (Exod

Table 11.1.

Exodus 1–4	John 4
The well	
Jacob, Joseph & their families: increasing numbers (*pleious eginonto,* 1:12) lead to oppression (chap. 1).	As Jesus makes more disciples (*pleionas . . . poiei*) he has to leave, and comes near Samaria to the land Jacob gave to Joseph (4:1, 5) . . .
The birth and saving of Moses (2:1–10).	?
Under pressure, Moses leaves for Midian and sits at a well (2:11–15).	. . . Coming to Jacob's well, Jesus sits on it (4:6).
The meeting with the women/woman	
The priest's daughters come to give drink to their sheep (2:16).	A woman comes from Samaria to draw water (4:7).
	The disciples were bringing food (4:8).
Because of hostile shepherds, Moses intervenes and gives the drink (2:17). Moses is to be invited to eat (2:18–20).	Jesus offers living water (4:10, 13–14).
The marriage	
Moses settles into a marriage (2:21–22).	
The prophetic revelation at the mountain	
Knowing the people's affliction, God proposes to lead them to worship, and reveals the holy name (2:23–3:15).	Aware of the woman's love plight, Jesus speaks of true worship, and reveals himself (4:16–26).
The mission	
Moses is to tell Israel. Israel will respond and, finally, go. A woman shall take spoils (3:16–22). *Signs, wonders, and faith* (Exod 4:1–26).	Leaving the jar, the woman goes and tells the people, and they go out to Jesus (4:28–30). [The official's son, John 4:43–54].
	The spiritual marriage (John 4:40). Jesus abides with the people. [As a groom with a bride, cf. 3:29.]
The people welcome the revelation	
Moses and Aaron tell the people. The people believe, glad that God has seen their distress (4:27–31).	The woman and Jesus tell the people. Many (more) believe (. . . *pleious*): "This is the Savior . . . (4:39–42).

1), and then, in a complementary text, it describes how, when the saved Moses tried to oppose the oppression, he had to leave Egypt and move to the land of Midian (Exod 2:1–15). The whole text (1:1–2:15) forms a subtle unity in which the increasing numbers finally lead to the flight of Moses.

In John there is a similar dynamic: because of increasing numbers of disciples and the implied hostility of the Pharisees, Jesus leaves Judea and comes to Samaria. Some of the similarity is quite detailed (see Table 11.2).

The Meeting with the Women/Woman and the Sharing of Drink, Food, and a Form of Marriage (Exod 2:16–20; John 4:7–15, 31–34, 40)

When Moses meets the women at the well he first gives water to their sheep, then he is invited to eat, and then he marries Zipporah. The same elements are present in John's account but in a spiritual form: the water which he gives is living water; his food is of another kind—to do the will of the one who sent him; and in place of the physical togetherness of marriage there is a picture of Jesus' abiding with those who believe in him. In John's preceding episode (3:22–36), the togetherness of Jesus and believers has already been described through the imagery of marriage.

The Prophetic Revelation at the Mountain (Exod 2:23–3:15, John 4:16–26)

To some degree, the essence of this similarity has already been dealt with. Knowing the slavery of the people/woman, the revealer first shows something which arouses a sense of surprise and wonder (the burning bush, Exod 2:23–3:6; prophetic knowledge, John 4:16–19) and then goes on to speak of salvation and worship (Exod 3:7–12, John 4:20–24). Next comes the revelation of identity (Exod 3:13–15, John 4:25–26), and it is done in such a way that John's formulation, though adapted to his own Christ-centered narrative, manages to contain within itself the key words of the older scene:

Exodus: *Egō eimi ho ōn.* ("I am who am.")
John: *Egō eimi ho lalōn soi.* ("I am [he] who am speaking to you.")

Table 11.2.

Exodus 2:15	John 4:1–6
"Pharaoh heard . . .	"When . . . the Pharisees heard . . .
so Moses withdrew from the face of Pharaoh	Jesus . . . left Judea
and transferred to the land of Midian.	and went away . . . through Samaria.
And coming to the land of Midian he sat on the spring" (2:15).	So coming to . . . Samaria . . . he sat . . . on the well" (4:1–6).

The Mission to the People (Exod 3:16–22, John 4:28–38)

Following the revelation of the divine name, the hesitant Moses is told to go and tell the people. The woman is not explicitly commissioned; instead the revelation itself arouses in her a spontaneous wish to bring it to others.

The Quest for Faith and Life, and the Role of Signs and Wonders (Exod 4:1–26, John 4:43–54)

Moses' subsequent conversations (4:1–26) are largely concerned with believing (4:1–9: "What if they will not believe?"), and with various forms of the threat of death (4:18–26: are his relatives still alive?, etc.). Within this context—belief and unbelief, life and death—there are several references to signs and wonders (esp. 4:8, 9, 17, 21).

What John apparently has done is use this text, particularly its emphasis on signs and wonders, to elaborate the account of the foreign official and his dying son (John 4:43–54, esp. v 48: "Unless you see signs and wonders . . ."). The full relationship between the texts seems to be quite complex.

The People Welcome the Revelation (Exod 4:27–31, John 4:39–42)

The final scene in the Exodus text is of Moses, now accompanied by Aaron, telling the message to the receptive people. In fact, Aaron takes over the transmission of the message. Similarly in John: the final scene is of the Samaritan woman telling the message to the people, but the transmission of the word is taken over by Jesus. It is as though Moses and the woman, despite the centrality of their prophetic roles, are ultimately simply mediators who facilitate a further form of communication. The people believe, and having reached this new level of communication with the divine word, they experience salvation. In Exodus (4:31) the idea of salvation is implied; in John (4:42) it is explicit.

John's Further Use of the Pentateuch

The dependence of John 4 on Exodus 1–4 is part of a larger pattern, one in which, in varying ways, John's entire gospel systematically distills and integrates the entire Pentateuch. As noted earlier, at times some aspects of the connection are fairly clear, particularly the beginning, middle and end—in the references to "the beginning" (Gen 1:1, John 1:1); in the account of feeding the people, especially with manna (Exod 16; John 6); and in the long closing discourse(s) (Deut 1–30, John 13–17). But having thus given out some signals of its thorough engagement with these other texts, the fourth gospel then procedes to use them in such a way that, generally speaking, the relationship is not immediately clear.

A full investigation of John's dependence on the Pentateuch lies beyond the scope of this study. What is given, in Appendix C, is simply an outline of that dependence. The outline is tentative but should be useful for further work.

John 4:1–42: Putting the Pieces Together

The picture which begins to emerge concerning the composition of John's text, or at least concerning 4:1–42, is that in writing this account the evangelist did indeed synthesize several Markan episodes—in other words, several episodes from the life of Jesus—but, having done that, he then set that synthesis in context, the context of the ancient experience of Israel (as reflected in the Pentateuch) and the context of the later experience of the church (Acts 8:1b–25).

At the same time, convinced of the involvement of the eternal savior in the details of human life, he has so presented Jesus that, even though Jesus speaks with eternal accents, his life and experience reflect the stages of a normal human life. Thus the various sources, as well as being blended, are profoundly reshaped to as to serve a new life-related purpose.

The result is a text in which several sources are present, all intricately interlocking and overlapping, but in which the finished narrative is something quite different from any of these sources. Jesus' meeting with the Samaritan woman captures the essence of the first prolonged encounters in Mark—with the troubled Gerasene and the life-seeking woman (Mark 5:1–20, 25–34)—but it elaborates that essence so that the woman is like a down-to-earth Moses, and it sets her on the stage of the city of Samaria. She reflects the earlier texts, yet she is someone quite new.

As well as using the passages already mentioned, John has also used other texts and sources. There is evidence, for instance, in the text of his knowledge of the area around Samaria. And there are several details which remain unaccounted for. As a partial answer to the question of what other sources John might have used it is appropriate now to touch on a further topic—the use of the epistles.

12

John's Systematic Use of Ephesians

Thus far John 17 has been linked, at least in passing, or through the appendices, with a wide variety of texts—the predeath prayer in Gethsemane (Mark 14:32–42; cf. Matt 26:36–46), the Our Father (Matt 6:9–13), the shepherdlike care for the little ones (Matt 18:10–14), the Zacchaeus incident (Luke 19:1–10), and Moses' final discourse (Deut 29–30). But despite the apparently genuine contribution of each of these component parts, John's climactic chapter appears to depend even more on yet another source—the epistle to the Ephesians.

Ephesians is concerned with how Christ brings the fragmenting world back to God. It is as though God's creation had come apart, riven by dark demonic sin, yet through an age-old plan of God—an eternal love, which comes from within God and which is manifested in Christ's self-giving—there is at work, even amid the world's darkness, a greater force for unity. Through this unifying power—a power which shows itself in the holiness and unity of the church—Christ is bringing creation to a new fulness.

This picture of God—as working through Christ to bring everything back to a greater unity—is central to John 17. When Jesus prays, his prayer implies a spiritual ascent which, even amid the world's evil, draws people towards holiness (17:6–19) and thereby towards unity—unity in God (17:20–26).

Ephesians consists essentially of two complementary sections, two views of what is ultimately a single process:

Chapters 1–3:   *God's eternal activity*, working through Christ and the church, of bringing everything to unity.

Chapters 4–6:   *The human response* which, inspired by Christ's ascent towards God, and especially by Christ's self-giving and care, cooperates in leaving evil aside and in working towards holiness and unity.

Between the two halves there is much complementarity and repetition. It would seem, for instance, as if both halves contain aspects of a threefold repetitive spiral (within chaps. 1–3, cf. 1:3–14, 1:15–2:10, 2:11–3:13; within 4–6, cf. 4:1–16, 4:17–5:5, 5:6–6:9), and as if the parts of the different spirals complement one another. Thus the mystery of Jews and Gentiles being united in the single body of Christ (cf. 2:11–3:13) is complemented by the mystery wherein Christ and the church, like man and wife, form a single body (cf. 5:6–6:9, esp. 5:22–33).

One aspect of this complementarity is that both halves build up towards a brief but striking passage—chapters 1 to 3 towards the picture of Paul falling on his knees and praying that people gain inner development, that by faith they come to the knowledge of God (3:14–21); and chapters 4 to 6 towards the picture of the inner battle, by which, particularly through faith and prayer, people ward off evil (6:10–20). Thus progress towards God, towards knowing God (3:14–21), is balanced by guarding against evil (6:10–20).

While the warding off of evil is important, it is not the epistle's primary concern. The picture which focuses Ephesians, and which

Table 12.1.

Ephesians 1–6	John 17
God's eternity-based secret of unity, Christ-mediated, in the church (1:1–3:13).	
I pray that by *knowing Christ you may be filled with God* (3:14–21).	The incarnation leads to a prayer that they *know God and Christ* (17:1–5).
Live accordingly—on the basis of Christ's unifying ascension to the father, his truth, his giving of himself for your sake, and his sanctifying action (chaps. 4–6).	*Jesus' ascentlike prayer* to the Father: may they *live accordingly*—in unity. For their sake, he sanctifies himself, in truth (17:6–19).
	Prayer for (church's) *unity, within God's eternal unity* (17:20–26).

stands quite literally at its center, is the positive one—that of Paul praying that despite evil, people should come, through Christ, to know God (3:14–21). Thus while the epistle does indeed consist of two balancing halves, this brief central picture has a certain priority of place and importance.

What John apparently has done is taken this central text (Eph 3:14–21) and set it in adapted form at the beginning of his chapter (17:1–5); and then he distills the rest of the epistle to form the remainder of the chapter. (See Table 12.1, p. 129.)

Aspects of a More Detailed Analysis

The Unity Which, Through Christ, Comes from God and Goes Back to God (Eph 1:1–3:13, John 17:20–26)

The discrepancy between the length and wording of these texts is so great that observations about the apparent dependence of one on the other must be tentative, at least in this brief analysis.

Ephesians is first concerned with how, within God's eternity, within God's primordial plan of love, unity began (1:3–14). The emphasis on beginnings is underlined in the Greek by the fact that several words start with *pro*, "before/pre-" ("*before* the foundation of the world," 1:4; "*predetermining* us, . . ." 1:5; cf. 1:9, 11, 12).

The text then goes on (1:15–3:13) to tell how this purposeful love flowed out as it were from God and, through Christ's forming of the church, started gathering fragmented humanity into a unified creation.

The conclusion of John 17 has a rather different focus. It looks, not so much at the place where unity began as, at the place to which it is going—the unity of the believers which culminates in final togetherness with Christ in God. In other words, John has adapted the distilled text to its new concluding position. Yet, even in thus looking forward, Jesus refers to the love which existed "before the foundation of the world" (17:24).

Despite being very different, the texts have some significant similarities. Apart from 1 Pet 1:20, the phrase "before the foundation of the world" (Eph 1:4, John 17:24) does not otherwise occur in the NT, and the similarity is strengthened by the fact that in the two instances the phrase is associated with both love and glory (Eph 1:4–6, John 17:24).

The Ephesians reference to "the . . . love with which [God] loved" (2:4) is unmatched in the NT—except for John 17:26.

Praying That the Believers/Disciples May Know God and Christ (Eph 3:14–21, John 17:1–5)

At this point John systematically transforms Ephesians, sentence by sentence almost (see Tables 12.2 and 12.3). Thus instead of one gesture of prayer (the bending of the knees) he uses another (the raising of the eyes). Instead of the idea of the inner self or inner person (*esō anthrōpos*), he speaks of eternal life. And in describing that inner reality he speaks not so much of a progression from knowing Christ to knowing (or experiencing) God, as of, first of all, knowing God and then, in second place, Christ.

In these initial adaptations (Eph 3:14–19, John 17:1–3) John generally follows the order of Ephesians, but he seems to have made one change: the emphasis on the universality of what God has wrought in Christ—from rootedness in Christ there is the development of *all the saints* and *a cosmic dimension* ("breadth, length, . . ." Eph 3:17–18)— this universality has been placed relatively earlier in John's text (in the reference to the fact that the Son has authority over *all flesh* and in a sense has been given "*all*," John 17:2).

In the later part of the texts, the Ephesians' emphasis on God being glorified in the church is replaced by the idea of God being glorified on the earth (Eph 3:20, John 17:4). And while Ephesians, as it comes to the end of a major section of the text, looks to an eternity which stretches into the future (Eph 3:21), John, whose chapter is beginning, manages a formulation which, while looking to the future (to the coming glory), also recalls the beginning ("before ever the world was," 17:5).

In Light of Jesus' Ascent and Self-Giving, Seek— Even Amid the World's Evil—To Live in Holiness and Unity (Eph 4:1–6:9, John 17:6–19)

In chapters 4–6 Ephesians becomes more practical: the mystery wrought in Christ is not just for admiration but for imitation. The text seems repetitious—as mentioned earlier it has aspects of a threefold spiral (4:1–16, 4:17–5:5, 5:6–6:9)—but it has two main threads: on the one hand, repeated appeals to live (literally to walk, *peripateō*) in unity

Table 12.2.

Prayer for an Inner Human Growth Which Is Based on Knowing God and All God Does in Christ

Ephesians 3:14–19	John 17:1–3
Paul prays . . . (3:14–15)	*Jesus prays . . .* (1a)
". . . I bend my knees	". . . Jesus raised his eyes
to the Father	to heaven
from whom every fatherhood in heaven . . .	and said, 'Father . . .
. . . for the inner self (3:16)	*. . . for eternal life* (for all) (17:1b–2)
Out of the richness of his glory	Glorify your Son that your Son may glorify you.
may he give you	As you have given him
power	authority
through his Spirit	over *all flesh* that to *all you have given him*
for the strengthening of your inner self	he may give eternal life.
Description of the inner self ("*with all*") (3:17–19)	*Description of eternal life* (17:3)
that Christ dwell through faith in your hearts, so that, rooted and	Now this is eternal life.
founded in love, you will have strength with *all the saints*, while	
grasping *the breadth, length, height, depth*.	
to know the knowledge-surpassing love of Christ	that they may know you, the one true God
and so be filled with all the fulness of God.	and him whom you have sent Jesus Christ

132

Table 12.3.

The Result of the Preceding Human Growth: God Is Glorified, and So Is Jesus	
Ephesians 3:20–21	John 17:4–5
God's work brings God glory . . . (3:20)	*God's work, done by Jesus, glorified God . . .* (17:4)
To him whose power can do infinitely more than we ask or think, working in us, to him glory in the church,	I have glorified you on the earth, having perfected the work which you gave me to do.
. . . glory in Jesus, eternally (3:21)	*. . . and brings Jesus an eternal glory* (17:5)
and in Christ Jesus for all generations, for ever and ever, Amen."	And now you glorify me Father with the glory I had with you before ever the world was.' "

and holiness, and, on the other, a series of pictures which develop the overall presentation of the work of Christ. Thus it speaks first of Christ as ascending and becoming a source of *unity* (4:7–13); then of Jesus reflecting *truth* and *giving himself for people's sake in sacrifice* (4:21–25, 5:2); and finally of Christ not only giving himself for others' sake—for the sake of the church—but also of his sanctifying the church, *making it holy* (5:25–27).

It is this latter series of pictures of Christ which John uses as a major component for the center of chapter 17—for its overall sense of an ascent and for its references to *unity*, *truth*, *self-giving* and *making holy*. To some degree these elements are spread right through John's text (17:6–19), but to a significant extent they have been gathered in a few climactic synthesizing verses at the end (17:17–19).

As often, there are some changes. When Ephesians speaks of Jesus' self-giving (5:2, 25), it refers clearly, at least in the first instance, to the idea of sacrifice. But in John's text (17:19) the explicit reference to sacrifice is omitted.

John also uses the more practical side of the epistle. In chapter 17, as in Ephesians, the ascension and saving goodness of Christ provide a context for referring to a positive human response, particularly to *keeping* what God has *given* (Eph 4:3, 7, 8, 11; John 17:6–9, 11–12). This is to be done amid a pagan world, a world which is in contrast with Christ

(Eph 4:17–19, John 17:14), and in which God must provide protection in the conflict with evil (Eph 6:10–20, John 17:15).

Conclusion

A full analysis of the relationship between Ephesians and the fourth gospel would require considerably more research. It would seem, for instance, that the image of washing and of mutual service (John 13) has affinities with the Ephesian image of bathing and of a service which is not equally mutual (Eph 5:22–33). Such affinities need careful analysis. But even at this stage an initial conclusion may be drawn. Given the broad but consistent similarities between the texts, and given particularly the precise relationship between the center of the epistle (Eph 3:14–21) and the beginning of John 17 (17:1–5), it seems reasonable to conclude that John had the epistle in hand and that he has used it in diverse ways as a major component of the entire chapter.

This does not necessarily mean that the epistle is a reliable guide to John's meaning. John adapted his sources—and also adapted their meaning. Ultimately interpretation relies on John's own text.

III

THE QUEST RESUMED: INITIAL CONCLUSIONS

13

The Religious Background

Probably the best working hypothesis is that, insofar as he was able, the evangelist used everything, or at least tested everything. The fact that his sources ranged from Genesis to Ephesians and that he used these sources systematically, suggests a process which was all-encompassing. This corroborates the view that John is to be seen against the background of first-century syncretism. Cullmann, for instance, had linked him with syncretistic Judaism (1976, 46–53, 89–91) and MacRae with syncretistic Hellenism (1970).

But syncretism does not do justice to the fourth gospel; it suggests an artificial unity, a combining of elements that, in fact, are alien to one another. John's unity was thorough and authentic. Much of his genius consisted of his ability to find the essence of his many sources and to see how, when rightly understood, they blended together.

This does not mean that his picture of unity is one of uniformity. For the evangelist, truth is complex; Barrett (1972, 49–69) would say it is dialectical. And so the gospel, even in its carefully crafted unity, is complex.

Rather than describe the evangelist as syncretistic it seems better to speak of him as encyclopedic—an encyclopedic theologian. Such an idea was not new. It followed a Jewish tradition which reached back to the composition of the Torah of Moses. As the Torah writers had sifted discriminatingly the cultures and traditions of their world and had then rewritten them in view of their own deepest insights, so the fourth evangelist perused all available writings and traditions, and then re-fashioned them in light of his own experience and purpose.

Given this wide-ranging approach it seems best, at least as a working hypothesis, to summarize John's use of background materials under three headings.

A Distillation of Canonical Writings

The present study has given indications of John's systematic use of the Torah, the synoptics, and Ephesians. However, it is not possible for the moment to say exactly how many canonical texts (OT and NT) John used. (Obviously when the fourth gospel was being written the NT canon was not yet fully formed, but within the early church certain Christian writings, which subsequently would become canonical, were probably already held in special regard.) Boismard has suggested that, apart from the synoptic gospels, John also knew some Pauline letters (1977, 47–48).

An Encyclopedic Distillation of Changing Judaism (Including Pre-Gnosticism)

Researchers have found so many threads between John and the changing Judaism of his day that he seems to have been aware of virtually every significant movement and to have sought to incorporate the essence of all that was best, including incipient gnosticism.

John's inclusion of pre-gnosticism was not as alien as it may sometimes seem. At their origins gnosticism and Christianity were closely related; both grew out of the OT. Pre-gnosticism's quest for knowledge, as found for instance at Qumran, "stood in the wisdom tradition of ancient Israel" (Fujita, 1986, 168). Many modern researchers (working on the theory of a sayings source, designated "Q") locate the sayings of Jesus within that same tradition. And even Luke's description (Acts 8:9–10) of Simon Magus, sometimes regarded as an early Gnostic, is colored by the OT description of the imposing Naaman (Brodie, 1986a, 48–50). If pre-gnosticism gleaned knowledge from the OT, Christianity involved a related gleaning—an effort to discover the heart of the OT, its spirit. In fact, rather than say that the two (Jesus and pre-gnosticism) are related, it seems more accurate to say that within Judaism, the prophetic emphasis on knowledge (e.g., Isa 1:3; Hosea 4:2,6; Jer 31:34) and the wisdom quest for understanding had helped to give birth to a single multifaceted search for spiritual knowledge. The complexity of this development is underlined by the fact that it is connected with the elusive origins of Jewish mysticism (Fujita, 1986, 158–84).

If aspects of pre-gnosticism were intertwined with the beginnings of the NT, it is, therefore, not surprising that several NT texts show traces of some forms of gnosticism. As Bultmann notes (1955, 6) such elements are found, for instance, in Paul. And it is widely agreed that they are found in Ephesians.

So when John uses language that is gnostic or pre-gnostic he is not importing something alien into the NT. Rather, to a large degree, he is clarifying and making explicit what is already there. The earlier NT writings had sought, in speaking of Jesus, to recapture the spiritual center of the OT. John takes that process a stage further—he makes the emphasis on the spiritual explicit.

Special attention has sometimes focused on John's theme of the descent and ascent, of a redeemer coming from God and returning to God. This does indeed have affinities with the gnostic redeemer myth as found in later documents, but it also has affinities with several canonical or Jewish documents—with wisdom's personification and entry into human life (cf. esp. Prov 8:22–9:6; Sir 24:1–31; Wis 7:22–8:1, 9:9–12), with Paul's image of the divine self-emptying (Phil 2:6–11), with various aspects of the Son of humanity and the atoning Servant (cf. Mark 10:45; for references, cf. Kysar, 1985, 2418), and with certain concepts of assumption or ascension (cf. 2 Kings 7:13, Luke 24:50–53, Acts 1:9–11, Hebrews 9).

Given this twofold affinity—with canonical or Jewish texts which *preceded* John, and with gnostic texts which, at least in their present form, *followed* him—the relative age of the various documents suggests that John's indebtedness is to the canonical or Jewish materials. This judgment is strengthened by the fact that, as is shown by the relationship of the fourth gospel to the Pentateuch, to the synoptics, and to Ephesians, John's general procedure was to absorb and synthesize precisely such older canonical/Jewish materials. In other words, his general practice of synthesizing explains how, on the basis of older canonical/Jewish materials he could have formulated the pattern of the descent and ascent.

As for the affinity with the gnostic idea of the redeemer, it would seem that the borrowing, insofar as it is present, is in the other direction: the gnostics borrowed from John. This is indicated not only by the lateness of the gnostic texts, but also by the fact that, in other matters, some of the gnostic texts definitely did borrow from John (Attridge, 1989).

As a general conclusion, therefore, it seems possible, as others have suggested, to distinguish between a fully developed gnosticism—one which, in many ways, is like an unbalanced derivation of Christianity— and an earlier complex movement, which went all the way from the heart of the OT, through various later Jewish writings, into the heart of the NT, and which, within its complexity, encompassed a form of pre-gnosticism, a pre-gnosticism which, in fact, was a type of mysticism.

Note: The Mandaeans

The Mandaeans are a religious sect who now live in Iraq. What is true of developed gnosticism is true also of them: their writings are late (c. 700 CE; they include references to Mohammed), and, insofar as they show affinity with John's gospel, the borrowing, if present, is in the other direction—*by* the Mandaeans, not *from* them (cf. Burkitt, 1928; Barrett, 41).

The detailed discussion of the origins of the Mandaeans and their literature is quite complex and inconclusive (cf. Baumgartner, 1950); by the nature of the case it is very difficult to prove the nonexistence of their gnostic traditions at the time the fourth gospel was written, and thus to exclude completely the possibility that they influenced the evangelist. Rather than attack this problem frontally, it seems better, at least for the moment, to work around it—to see to what extent John's dependence on known, controllable documents, such as the canonical texts, provides an alternative explanation which is more convincing.

A Deliberate Engagement with Hellenism

At first sight it may seem that John would have little to do with Hellenism. His massive dependence on Judaism could be seen as excluding such an interest. Besides, Hellenism was the culture of "the world"— something to which the fourth gospel was opposed. It is easy, therefore, to imagine a sharp division between John and pagan Hellenism.

Yet the weight of evidence suggests otherwise. Precisely because it was the dominant world culture, Hellenism needed to be engaged. However deep the gospel's antagonism towards the world, its first emphasis was on God's love for the world (3:16). And in various ways the idea of a positive mission towards the world is repeated in the gospel— for instance, in the movement from emphasizing Jerusalem to emphasizing Galilee, and in the climactic references both to the hope that the world would believe (17:21–23) and to the universal symbol of the 153 fish (21:11). If the world was the object of so much love and interest, there is no way that its culture could have been treated with indifference. Hellenism would indeed have been subjected to incisive criticism, but it would also have been treated with deep sympathy.

Such an interest in Hellenism would not have been excluded by John's dependence on Judaism. On the contrary, despite the presence in Judaism of some sectarian groups, its primary tradition was one of thorough engagement with the world's culture. This is true of books ranging all the way from Genesis and Exodus (with their sundry dependencies on Mesopotamian stories and Egyptian literary traditions) to such writings as Proverbs and the Book of Wisdom (with their various dependencies on Egyptian wisdom literature and on other aspects of Egyptian culture).

That tradition of engagement was not forgotten in John's day. Indeed it could not be forgotten, for on every side Hellenism confronted Judaism daily, and often pervaded it. There was no way that a writer who was seeking to make a new synthesis of Jewish tradition could fail to engage the culture which surrounded it and which, while enriching it, threatened to engulf it.

It seems best, therefore, when assessing the affinities noted earlier, between John and Hellenism, to see them not as minor details, but as telltale signs of a serious engagement with contemporary culture. Such a viewpoint helps not only to set these details in perspective; it also provides some added context for the investigation of other affinities.

Assessing John's engagement with Hellenism would be somewhat easier if it were known to what extent other NT writers were so engaged. But so far the practice of these earlier writers is not fully clear. It is only now beginning to emerge, for instance, to what extent Paul engaged the philosophical questions of his day (cf. Malherbe, 1989). If it is established that Paul was involved in such a process, then the idea of a somewhat similar engagement by John is more likely, particularly if John used Paul.

14

The Purpose/Life-Situation

In light of the gospel's unity and of its dependence on diverse canonical writings it is now possible to assess the view that it was written for some narrow audience or purpose—for a synagogue-centered conflict with Jews, for a Samaritan mission, or as an anti-docetic polemic. All of these elements are present in some way—Jewish conflict, Samaritan mission, and an emphasis on the Word made flesh—yet they are but parts of a larger whole. They are part of a mission which, though it included outcast Samaria and was interested in it, went far beyond it; a mission which, however anguished by the break with Judaism, was governed primarily by positive concerns; a mission in which the picture of the Word as flesh was but part of a larger account of God's thoroughgoing and purposeful involvement with humankind. These hypotheses, though they capture an aspect of the gospel, do not explain its purpose.

There is no way, for instance, that the hypothesis of a conflict within a synagogue—at least as formulated thus far—can allow for John's use of the synoptics and Ephesians. The hypothesis depends on reading the gospel as springing from within the inner dynamics of a synagogue community—first, from its preaching, and then, from its dividedness. Once it is seen that the evangelist used a rich diversity of sources, that hypothesis is no longer usable. Its lasting value is not that it explained the purpose of John's gospel but that it highlighted one of its elements.

John's actual purpose would seem to have been that of making an appeal to all Christians, regardless of the diversity of their backgrounds. This has generally been the popular view, and in recent times has been corroborated by a significant number of scholars (C. K. Barrett, G.

MacRae, J. Schneider P. Lamarche, R. Longenecker, R. E. Brown; for references, see Kysar, 1985, 2430–31).

This universality of purpose is indicated by two main factors— universality of sources, and universality of applicability. Concerning John's sources their full range is not yet known, but even at this stage they show such a wide diversity that they imply an interest which is universal.

Universality of applicability refers to the fact that to a significant degree the gospel is organized on a basis which appeals to everyone— that of the structure of a human life. Furthermore it has been shown throughout the centuries, in thousands of diverse social settings, that this gospel does, in fact, have an extraordinarily wide appeal. If it frequently confronts the unbelieving Jews, that does not make it narrow, for "Jews" has a further wider meaning, and the confrontation or challenge applies to everybody. The characters in the gospel are such that, when one pauses to assess one's life, one or another of these characters can act as a mirror, critical yet sympathetic, for the state of one's soul. It was not without reason that, for a long period in the life of much of the church, the prologue was read at every eucharist. And it is not without reason that, as Hoskyns (20) implies, John's gospel may be read to all, including the poor and the dying.

15

Questions About the Reality of the Johannine Community: Towards Seeing the Evangelist as Primarily an Integrated Member of the Larger World-Oriented Christian Community or Church

As seen earlier, there is considerable diversity in the various reconstructions of "the history of the Johannine community." This does not mean that these reconstructions are without value. On the contrary, each captures some aspect of the gospel. Yet the diversity is sufficiently deep that it raises serious questions about the entire undertaking.

The most basic question is whether such a community ever existed. Obviously the evangelist lived somewhere and presumably had some friends and acquaintances—but that does not constitute a distinct community.

Two factors have contributed significantly to the idea of a community which was distinct: the fact that the fourth gospel is distinct—even to the point, some would say, of having an independent historical tradition—and the general presupposition, going back especially to Gunkel (1901) and filtered through the early form-critics, that biblical narratives originate, not so much from individual writers, as from the complex workings of communities. These elements need to be examined.

An Independent Historical Tradition?

John is distinct in several ways, but most of all at the basic level of plot—the level which tells the story of Jesus. John's story is independent, quite distinct from the synoptics; and so the hypothesis has been put forward that John relied on an independent historical tradition (see esp. Dodd, 1963). Once it became credible that, apart from the mainline tradition of the synoptics, there was another tradition which was independent, then it was plausible to suggest that the distinct tradition was based in a distinct community.

But the historical tradition found in John is not independent. The reliance on the synoptics is pervasive. What is independent is John's reshaping of the tradition, his reworking of it in order to develop his theological vision. In his own way he was just as closely involved with Matthew, Mark, and Luke as they were with one another. Thus the idea of an independent historical tradition is left without its foundation.

This implies that in the quest for the historical Jesus, John makes no perceptible contribution. If he reflects the historical Jesus he does so only to the extent that he reflects aspects of whatever may be historical in the synoptics.

If there is no tradition of independent history then the hypothesis of an independent community becomes less necessary.

And what applies to history may be applied also to other aspects of the gospel, particularly to its theology: the independence, though real, requires very little explanation other than the evangelist's creativity in reworking diverse sources and forming a new synthesis.

Yet a doubt lingers. Some of the reconstructions have been so vivid that, like well-known novels or television series, they take on a life of their own, and even though one knows they are not historical, they live on in the imagination, and so retain their hold. Besides, the Gunkel-inspired presupposition about the role of communities will not be easily dispelled. In fact, some recent developments in the social sciences have tended to strengthen it. It is necessary therefore to look further.

A Community Production?

The social sciences provide important reminders that documents do not come out of the void; in varying degrees they reflect the contemporary situation in society, and, in varying degrees, by reading them carefully it is possible to discern something about their social setting. This is true also of the fourth gospel; it reflects aspects of a specific social situation, and, to that extent at least, it reflects a specific community.

But that need not mean either that the community was narrow, or that the community was the primary force in composing the gospel. There is nothing, in principle, which prevents the community from being the whole human race. And there is nothing, in principle, which prevents the writer, despite an acute awareness of all of humanity, from being highly individualistic.

An examination of the fourth gospel shows that not only in principle but also in practice these two possibilities are worth considering. John's language, for instance, despite its puzzles, consisted of a simple form of Koine Greek, and so was as close as one could come to a language that was universal. The prologue evokes God's involvement with all of humanity. Both the gospel's first words of dialogue and the first words spoken by Jesus have a dimension which is at once simple and universal: "Who are you?" (1:19); "What do you seek?" (1:38). There is a similar universality in John's first most distinctive characters, Nicodemus and the woman of Samaria: they summarize many of the foundational preoccupations and divisions of the world—career and love-life, Jew and non-Jew, man and woman.

It is true, of course, that much of John is specific, even detailed. The prologue alludes to division, the verb "seek" has a technical meaning, and the scene at Samaria contains local color. But specifics and details do not take away from universality. Details give life to literature; in Nabokov's phrase, "The detail is everything" (cf. Alter, 1985, 3). Similarly with specifics: a story may be local, but it may also be of universal import. The fact that it is localized, far from destroying its universal appeal, very often strengthens it.

In dealing with John, and in asking what social world he reflects, the difficulty is to find a balance between the universal and the specific, and also between different specifics. It is easy, in reading literature, to let one element get out of balance. Because the life of James Joyce, for instance, has been so well chronicled, it is generally known that *Ulysses* is concerned with universal human experience and was written in cosmopolitan Zurich, where Joyce was living with his beloved common-law wife. But *Ulysses* is set in Dublin and occasionally reflects the wording of the Catholic Mass—so much so that at one level it is possible to speak of "*Ulysses* as Missal" (Harrigan, 1984). It would be easy then, if one were writing centuries after Joyce, and if his life were unchronicled, to be misled by the allusions to the Mass: Joyce was a cult writer, presumably a priest who was attached to one of the Dublin churches; someone who in writing *Ulysses* drew on the experience of a life-long ministry among Dublin's marginalized, probably in the colorful northern side of the city. Parts of the book do not fit this thesis, but they were put in by later editors, particularly by the Sensuous Redactor. It is the process of redaction which has made the book confused. The social world which is revealed is that of a Dublin parish at the turn of the century.

To some degree this is true. *Ulysses* does reveal much about Dublin at the turn of the century. Joyce not only remembered accurately; he would even write home from Zurich to check details of location.

But the location was peripheral to his central concern, to the fact that the primary reality with which he wrestled and which he sought to address was human life in general. The allusions to the Mass were included because, as well as being specific, they reflected a larger experience. The missal from which they were taken was but one of the many far-reaching sources, ancient and modern, through which the author sought to explore the depths of life.

Similarly in assessing the social world of John. It is easy, particularly after invoking hypothetical redactions, to take one aspect and reconstruct it into a social world, a community. Such reconstructions may contain some truth, yet they run the risk of obscuring something which is more important, namely that the primary community which impinged on the evangelist was far wider.

The process of misconstrual which has been applied to John's gospel—using the supposed independence of the gospel to recontruct a supposedly independent community—has been applied also to the Johannine epistles (1, 2, and 3 John). In fact, it is precisely the epistles-based reconstructions that Childs (1985, 483) describes as coming from creative imagination rather than historical controls. The Elder's condemnation of the power-hungry Diotrephes (3 John 6–11), for example, may seem at first sight to describe part of the history of a specific community. But the hunger for power haunts all human societies— "Power is the main temptation for church leaders" (O'Leary, 1991)— and, despite the matter-of-fact appearance of the text, it is not easy to determine whether the condemnation is meant to address a local situation or whether it is meant rather as a universal warning.

A similar ambiguity occurs in the gospel concerning the figure of Peter. The fourth evangelist went to great lengths to show Peter, the holder of high office, as subject to controls (subject not only to his own weaknesses, but dependent also on the Spirit-like beloved disciple: John 13:23–24, 20:1–10, 21:7). It was the gospel's way of declaring that the ultimate power in God's realm is not an office-holder but the Spirit of love. And so the portrait of Peter is ambiguous: though it is primarily concerned with a general theological truth (the primacy of love over power), it reads as if it were history. In fact, few things could be more vivid or history-like than the scenes in which Peter is with the beloved disciple. Yet it is very difficult to rely on these scenes as a basis for reconstructing the specific episodes of Peter's life.

So when, in 3 John, one finds a contrast between the loving Elder and the abusive Diotrephes, one does not know whether it is history or a general warning. If the gospel is to be one's guide, and if one takes seriously the kinship between the gospel and the epistle, then it is likely that the Elder-Diotrephes contrast has a general theological purpose. It is questionable, therefore, whether it can ever be a fruitful exercise to attempt to reconstruct the history of Diotrephes. And the same applies to other elements in the Johannine epistles. The approach, which placed undue emphasis on the fourth gospel as historical (rather than theological), has also tended to misread the Johannine epistles. What is needed now is not further detail in reconstruction but a clearer sense of the very nature of these documents.

Obviously the Johannine writings constitute a distinct grouping within the NT. But distinctness does not demand literary independence, still less, physical separation (separateness of community). If the fourth gospel, despite its distinctness, is so thoroughly interwoven with the other gospels, then there is no reason why the Johannine writings as a whole may not be discovered to be similarly interwoven with the other NT writings.

It is reasonable therefore to visualize the writer(s) of the Johannine literature as engaged with the entire Christian community and with the place of that community in the entire world.

Yet, in a positive sense, the evangelist was also individualistic. The fourth gospel was not written by a series of redactors or by someone who edited sundry sermons. Not only is it distinct; it is a tightly wrought artistic unity in which every detail is chiselled into complex coordination with several other details. Many people around him may have made suggestions, but the final product is best explained as the work of a single writer, insightful and disciplined.

Putting Some of the Pieces Together

As has sometimes been implied or suggested (Fischer, 1975, 290–98; Kysar, 1985, 2425; and esp. Hengel, 1989, ix) the most important missing link in modern Johannine research appears very clearly to be the creativity of the evangelist himself. He has been underestimated—even by those who valued him. In ancient times he may not have been fully understood, but at least his status was higher. He was The Theologian, the inspired writer whose soaring vision was symbolized in the eagle. Why he has been less esteemed in modern times is difficult to say and probably involves several factors, among them the realization that apparently he was not John the beloved disciple, the emphasis on history rather than theology, on communities and redactors rather than authors, and also perhaps a subtle presupposition of modern superiority. (In the nineteenth and twentieth centuries it has sometimes been implied that biblical writers were primitive or naive [e.g., see S. Warner, 1979]. And one modern commentator implies that today's scholarship has detected a unity within one of the synoptics which John, if he had had the text, would not have seen—as though modern scholarship knew more about the gospels than one of the evangelists themselves.) There is the further important factor that even in premodern times the gospels were cut off from their literary context, and thus from a world in which some degree of creativity was taken for granted. In any case, whatever the full explanation, the evangelist appears to have had more creative genius— literary and theological—than has generally been recognized. He stands out then, more than formerly, in his individuality.

It is difficult to judge how people first reacted to his gospel. In the surviving church documents of the first half of the second century a number of writers seem to allude to John—at least they show affinities with him—but they do not refer to him directly (cf. Schnackenburg, 2:196–98). However, around 175 CE, or soon afterwards, John is reflected explicitly and in triple form: in the way his status as one of the four normative gospels is presupposed (as witnessed in the *Diatessaron of Tatian*); in the first extant direct quotation (by Theophilus of Syrian Antioch, an apologist bishop—cf. Schnackenburg, 1:199; Dubois, 1980); and in the first commentary (by Heracleon, a gnostic).

Heracleon's commentary was but one manifestation of the gnostic enthusiasm for John (cf. Pagels, 1989)—an enthusiasm which has tended to reinforce the hypothesis of a marginal evangelist and a marginal Johannine community.

But that explanation is not necessary. The fact that a commentary on John by a church writer was not composed until fifty years after Heracleon's (Origen's, c. 225), does not mean that within the church John's status was in serious doubt. (Apparently there was no commentary on Mark—apart from some compilations—until the seventh century [Kealy, 1982, 28, 36]).

There is another explanation which is more plausible. As already noted, John was highly individualistic, with a major element of creative genius. Creative genius is difficult to absorb. The difficulty for the early church was all the greater because in the fourth gospel the word "church" is never mentioned, and because, at one level, the traditional church leader, Peter, is made secondary to a character who is not highlighted in the other gospels. What John effectively had done, done more clearly than the synoptics, was challenge the church to place the spiritual not only above the material, but also, at one level, above the organizational.

Such is the stuff of saints, and it rejuvenates the inner heart of the church. But it requires a delicate balance, a realization that though the spiritual is primary, it is also like the Word—incarnated in things of flesh, in human realities involving material and organization. It would be easy for someone with gnosticizing tendencies to seize on John's emphasis on the spiritual and to take it out of context. Such, in fact, is what the gnostics did, and it must have meant that John's message, challenging by its very nature, became even more difficult to hear attentively.

In any case, there are two solid facts: John is grounded in the mainline tradition as found in the synoptics; and it is in the mainline tradition, as one of the four canonical gospels, that John finally remains. The fact that his work was abused by some, and may perhaps have been resisted or passed over by others, does not make him marginal and does not require the hypothesis of a distinct community. (The Second Vatican Council, for instance, was variously abused and resisted, but that did not make it marginal).

John emerges then as a challenging voice from within the heart of the Christian church. He was marginal only insofar as any prophet, by the simple fact of being a prophet, is marginal. His sense of community apparently contained at least two levels—a solidarity with the church at large and presumably a more specific solidarity with those around him. Who exactly was in this closer group is difficult to say, but perhaps the one word which cannot be used to describe it is "Johannine." Such a word suggests exclusiveness, whereas the composition of his gospel indicates the opposite—a close interaction with other NT writers. Whether this interaction was based simply on good communications or whether all these writers lived in the same area (community? school?) seems difficult to say, at least for the moment.

Concerning John's attitude towards the world and towards the Jews there seems to have been a deep ambivalence. Ideally the whole world was John's community; as already noted the gospel emphasizes a positive mission towards the world—God's sending of the Son and the Son's sending of the believers (cf. esp. 3:16, 17:20–23, 20:21–23, 21:11). But the world, in various ways, is destructive and so has to be resisted.

This resistance to the world has sometimes been interpreted as a thorough rejection of the world, and, as such, has been used, along with other factors, to say that Christianity, particularly in its Johannine form, constituted a sect. Such a judgment, however, is unbalanced; it does not take account of the more positive data. The church did indeed resist the world, but it also saw the world as loved, and it went out to it.

Some recent studies have begun to recognize this complexity. Rensberger, for instance, holds that the Johannine community was a sect (Rensberger, 1988, 28), but he grants, particularly because of the work of Onuki (1984), that its sectarianism "is not a pure example" (Rensberger, 1988, 144). The unsuitability of the term "sect" is increased by fact that many of the sectarian attitudes attributed to the hypothetical Johannine community are based on a misreading of the gospel—on a separating of John from the synoptics, on a bypassing of the gospel's theology, and on a projection of polemic.

John also shows ambivalence, though of a different kind, towards the Jews. Insofar as he perceives them as having rejected the Word of life he uses them as symbols of unbelief, and thus as symbols of the way in which the human spirit becomes negative about life and chooses various forms of death. On the other hand, in such episodes as those involving Nathanael (1:45–51) and Mary Magdalene (20:11–18), the evangelist has indicated an undercurrent of hope—that the Jews will find renewed optimism and openness.

Overall, therefore, the evangelist emerges not as the leader of an independent group but as a prophetic voice from within the church—a voice critical of the world, critical in another way of the Jews, and critical in yet a further way of the church and its leadership (Peter); but a voice which, even amid so much darkness, never failed to reflect a vision of light and life—for the church, for the Jews, and for the world.

General Conclusion:
From History to Spirit

According to the well-known saying which is attributed to Clement of Alexandria, the fourth evangelist moved gospel composition from an emphasis on external events to an emphasis on the world of spirit (Eusebius, *HE* 6.14.7). To a lesser degree that is also the effect of the present study: in conjunction with the present writer's commentary, it helps to move the study of the gospels, or at least of the fourth gospel, from a search for history to a search for spirit.

Credit for this transition, from history to spirit, must go ultimately to the historical method itself. Had it not been for the historical-critical insistence that, as a straightforward narrative, the text is confused, there would have been little incentive to look beyond the straightforward level and thus to discover that coherence lies primarily at the level of spirit and of spiritual stages.

The move away from history refers to the fact that the fourth gospel, as here understood, does not help in solving two specific historical problems, namely, the quest for the historical Jesus and the quest for the history of a distinct Johannine community. Concerning Jesus, John's story is highly distinctive, but it is so governed by aims which are literary and theological, and is so dependent on the synoptics, that it may be called historical only insofar as it contains elements of whatever is historical in the synoptics. Similarly concerning the idea of a distinct Johannine community: the gospel is so universal—both in its sources and in its applicability—that it is best seen not as the product of a distinct community, still less as that of a sect, but as a reflection—a distinctive reflection—of the central Christian tradition, a tradition which, in dealing with the world, simultaneously resisted it and went out to it.

But despite the move away from these two quests, investigation of the fourth gospel can still contribute to historical research.

It contributes, in the first place, towards recovering a sense of the evangelist. It does not reveal his identity, but it shows that he was in contact with other NT writings (writers?), and it gives an idea of the process of composition. It was not written quickly. Renée Bloch at one point (1957, 1271) describes the OT Chronicler as producing, in his own way, "a meditation on history." So also, though in a very different way, the fourth evangelist wrote a work of meditation. He has assembled wide-ranging sources and has synthesized them through a process which combines precise technique with heartfelt vision.

The foregoing analysis of the fourth gospel contributes also towards questioning a widespread idea of fragmentation. This fragmentation is of various kinds: within the gospel (by saying that the various parts do not really fit together); between John and the other gospels (by saying John is independent of them); and between all four gospels and literature at large. Ultimately all these hypotheses of disconnectedness are of a piece; they are all based on the difficulty of appreciating the sophisticated literary nature of the text. It is lack of literary appreciation, combined with a focus on history rather than on spirit, which fails to see the connectedness of John's diverse sections and styles. It is lack of appreciation for a further aspect of literary practice—that of rewriting or imitating existing texts—which fails to connect John to the synoptics. And ultimately it is the same general problem—the failure to appreciate the gospels as literary—which means that in relation to literature the gospels as a whole become cut off.

Once literary appreciation is restored, and once the disciplined creativity of the evangelist is recognized, these scattered pieces may be brought together. The result is a picture in which some of the NT writers, instead of being scattered in isolated marginal communities, begin to appear much closer to one another and much closer to the culture of the day.

Thus, historically speaking, there is both loss and gain. The image of a distinct Johannine community may have faded, but other images have become clearer—that of the individual evangelist, and, to some degree, that of the larger church, or at least, that of the cultural awareness and literary coordination among some of the church's leading prophetic writers.

Yet the fundamental reality reflected in the gospel is more than history, more than something cultural or literary. It is spiritual; it is an exploration and exposition of the spiritual world which the story of Jesus revealed. Of all realities it is the most important and the most elusive.

Its importance is seen especially in the freedom with which the evangelist reshaped the synoptic narratives in order to give a clearer portrait of the working of the Spirit. This freedom is a way of saying that at a certain level what counts in the heritage of Christianity is not the guarding of a past history but the discovering of a present spiritual reality.

And that reality is elusive. It was received, apparently, by a nameless disciple who came for a day and abode with Jesus (1:35–39). But not by Nicodemus, the leading intellectual authority—a reminder that study alone and authority alone do not grasp it. Nor does the writing of commentaries necessarily do so—not even the writing of books about origins.

APPENDIX A

The Story of the Adulteress
and the Accusers: John 7:53–8:11

53Then each one went away home; 1but Jesus went to the Mountain of Olives. 2Early in the morning he was there again in the temple, and all the people came to him. And he sat and taught them.

3But the scribes and Pharisees brought a woman who had been caught in adultery, and standing her in the middle, 4they said to him, "Teacher, this woman was caught in the very act of adultery. 5Now in the law, Moses commanded us to stone such women. And you—what do you say? 6This they said tempting him that they might have something with which to accuse him. But Jesus bent down and with his finger began writing on the ground.

7When they continued asking him, he straightened himself up and said to them, "Let the one who is without sin among you be the first to throw a stone at her." 8And again bending down he wrote on the ground. 9But they hearing this went away one by one, beginning with the elders.

And he was left alone, with the woman still before him. 10Then straightening himself up Jesus said to her, "Woman, where are they? Has no one condemned you?" 11She said, "No one, Lord." Then Jesus said to her, "Neither do I condemn you. Go your way, and do not sin again."

Comment

This passage did not belong to the original gospel. It is not in the oldest Greek manuscripts. And in some of the later manuscripts, when it is included, there are notes to indicate its uncertainty. A few manuscripts locate it elsewhere—after John 21:25, or after Luke 21:38. (For details and references, see esp. Schnackenburg, 1:181–82).

Despite its secondary nature the story seems to be old. According to the research of U. Becker (1963, 150–64), it would appear to have come from Jewish-Christian circles in the second century and to have been included with the gospels at the beginning of the third century. Its subsequent inclusion in the most popular translation of the Western church (St. Jerome's Latin Vulgate) ensured its permanent place in church tradition. It stands on the margin between what is canonical and noncanonical.

To a limited degree this marginal text is based on a kindred text which is almost equally marginal—the story of Susanna, a story which in the (Greek) Septuagint is attached to the book of Daniel and which is sometimes reckoned as Daniel 13. The Susanna story is much longer, and it concerns a woman who is innocent, yet the links are significant: the authorities (the two judges in Daniel 13; the scribes and Pharisees in John) use an accusation of adultery not to seek justice but to pervert it (to vent their frustrated desire of abusing Susanna physically; to abuse Jesus spiritually). But the evil purpose is thwarted: Daniel intervenes and shows that it is the judges who are sinful; and Jesus brings out the sinfulness of the scribes and Pharisees. In the end the women go free: Susanna is acquitted of any shamefulness, and the adulteress goes away to sin no more.

Apart from these general similarities there are also some similarities of detail, for instance, the departure of each for his own house (Dan 13:13, John 7:53), and the emphasis on the fact that (some of) the accusers were elders (*presbyteroi*, Dan 13:5, 8, 16, 19, etc.; John 8:9).

Given this link with Daniel 13 it seems likely that some other aspects of the adulteress story (the temple, the bending *down* and straightening *up*, and the writing on the ground) are partly influenced by Daniel 5 (abuse of the temple vessels, the humbling of those who raised themselves up, and the writing on the wall). In other words, as was partly suggested by some of the examples taken from Fishbane's analysis of Jewish methods of interpretation (1985, 250), two ancient texts (Daniel 13 and 5) seem to have been synthesized.

Whatever the details, and however great the influence of the Daniel passages, the story of the adulteress is essentially Christian. In contrast to the scribes and Pharisees, it shows Jesus as overcoming the weight of the sinful past and the weight of petty prestige games. Whether or not the writing on the ground is a variation on the writing on the wall—and thus an intimation that the reign of the scribes and Pharisees is coming to an end—it certainly has about it a refreshing quality of something which is both humble and puzzling, something which issues a quiet challenge to high-and-mighty accusers. It is a way of communicating one of the most basic aspects of the message of Jesus—that even for those sunken in shame, there is at hand, in a way legalists cannot imagine, a world of understanding and mercy.

APPENDIX B

John's Use of Names

One feature of John's distinctive plot is his distinctive use of names. This does not mean that John is independent of the synoptics; as already seen he relies heavily on the earlier gospels. Yet he uses them in an independent way, a way which serves his own literary and theological purposes, and as part of that independent usage he sometimes employs different names.

The purpose of this appendix is to look at some of these names and thus to gain a closer view of some of the evangelist's procedures. The names refer to both people (e.g. Nathanael, Nicodemus, Lazarus, Malchus) and places (e.g. Bethany beyond the Jordan, Cana, Aenon near Salim, a town of Samaria called Sychar, the five-portico pool called Bethzatha, the pool of Siloam, the portico of Solomon [cf. Acts 3:11], a town, near the desert, called Ephraim, a place called Stone-pavement).

An examination of some of these names leads to two initial conclusions. On the one hand John had independent information concerning the setting—for instance, concerning the five-portico pool, which has now been excavated. On the other hand, despite being well informed, despite knowing the geography (and topography) in a unique way, he would appear to have repeatedly subjected geographic interests, including geographic names, to his theological purposes. The sea of Galilee, for instance, is referred to as the "sea of Galilee of Tiberias" (6:1)—a name which is awkward but which has a connotation of universality appropriate to the theme of chapter 6.

"Aenon near Salim" (3:23), insofar as it means "Springs near Peace" is also theologically appropriate. Likewise "Ephraim" (11:54), which means "fruitful" and is close to the desert, introduces the theme of the grain which dies and bears much fruit. The reference to Bethany beyond the Jordan (1:28) sets up a situation where, at the time of the crisis involving Lazarus, the reason Jesus is not in Bethany [near Jerusalem] is because he is in Bethany [beyond the Jordan] (cf. 1:28; 10:40; 11:1, 18]—an ambiguity which is perfectly suited to the Lazarus story: it suggests, when death strikes, that the Lord, who apparently is absent, in fact is present.

A further factor is worth noting. Most of the cities or towns peculiar to John are largely or totally unknown to geographers—Bethany beyond the Jordan, Aenon near Salim, Sychar, Ephraim. Thus while the theological dimension of John's cities is strong, their hold on history is often fragile.

One feature is particularly curious and probably deserves further research: John's names tend at times to blend into one another. For instance, while the burial account is preceded by a reference to Jos-*eph* of *Ar-im*-athea (John 19:38), the Bethany anointing, which intimates the burial, is preceded by a reference to the elusive *Eph-ra-im* (John 11:54). There is something similar in the names and titles of the women. In Greek, *Martha is very close to Maria*; the only difference is between theta and iota, letters which are next to one another in the alphabet. *Ma-r-tha* is also related to *Tho-ma-s*; again *r* and *s* are beside one another in the Greek alphabet. (These names appear for the first time in the story of Lazarus [John 11:1–16]). The continuity goes further in the names at the cross—*Maria Kl-ōpas* and *Maria M-agdalēnē* John 19:25); again, *kl* and *m* follow one another in the alphabet; and both follow theta and iota: *th, i, k, l, m.* Blended puzzlingly with *Maria Klōpas* and *Maria Magdalēnē* are Jesus' mother and the sister of his mother. His mother is called "woman" (19:26; cf. 2:4)—the title given to the woman of Samaria (4:21). Apart from a few other brief references—the metaphorical bride (John 3:29), the woman in childbirth (16:21), and the fateful doorkeeper (18:16–17)—these are the only women in the gospel.

The general impression which emerges is that while John did indeed have special information concerning the setting, his governing interest was in his literary and theological purpose. To this, other interests were subordinated, including the use of names.

APPENDIX C

John's Use of the Pentateuch:
A Tentative Outline of One Dimension

The following outline reflects the fact that John's gospel depends systematically on the sequence of the Pentateuch. However, this sequential dependence does not account fully for John's use of the Pentateuch; many reworkings of the ancient text occur outside of this scheme. This is particularly true in the final stages of the gospel, when Jesus' death becomes the occasion for depicting dramas of sin (18:1–19:16a) and creation (19:16b–chap. 20), and when the dependence, as well as being on the end of the Pentateuch, on the account of the death of Moses, is also on its beginning—on the Genesis narratives concerning creation and sin. Consequently the outline, instead of reflecting John's complete engagement with Moses, reflects one aspect of it.

Genesis	John	Connection
1:1–2:4a	1:1–18	The essential goodness of God's creation.
2:4a–chap. 3	1:19–34	The opening trial (failed in Genesis, passed in John) and the decisive animal (the serpent/the lamb). Regarding not untying the shoes, out of reverence; cf. Moses' reverential removal of his shoes (Exod 3:5). Thus in both texts God is awesomely present, but in the gospel God is wearing shoes.
4:1–16(3:7–8)	1:35–51	Closeness (or lack of closeness) with the divine (with God/Jesus)

		and its effect on the relationship with one's brother (Cain and Abel, Andrew and Peter). In a state of apparent alienation, people are withdrawn (the man and the woman among the trees, wearing fig-leaves; Nathanael under a fig tree).
4:17–chap. 5	2:1–11?	The withering of life (morally, as reflected in civilization's descent into Lamech's type of brutality; physically, as seen in the implacable descent of the patriarchs into death; at Cana, as seen in the failure of the wine), and the revival of life through communication with the divine (by Enoch, Enosh and Noah; by Mary and the attentive servants at Cana).
6:1–9:17	2:12–22	The cleansing (of humankind; of the symbol-laden temple). The suggestion (within John's context of the language of descent and ascent) of a life or sojourn of few days (Gen 6:1–4, John 2:12–13). Disrupting corrupt human life and making an instrument of purification (Gen 6:5–chap. 7, the ship; John 2:14–16, the whip). Remembering, reconstructing humanity (through the deluge, through Jesus' death), giving a sign, and again remembering (Gen 8:1–9:17, John 2:17–22).
9:17–chap. 11	2:23–25?	The emptiness of a merely human knowledge of life; ultimate human bankruptcy (cf. Gen 11:10–32, increasingly short lives, barrenness and premature death all indicate the fading of life and the supremacy of death).

12:1–25:18	3:1–21	Against the background of the preceding bankruptcy, the story or challenge of a birth which comes from God (the process of birth which culminates in Isaac and in Abraham's abandonment to a surpassing God; and the birth offered to Nicodemus).
25:19–chap. 50	3:22–36?	The story or evoking of a complete life (Jacob/John) and of someone who, towards the end of life, is ready to let go of it because of having seen something greater (cf. Gen 46:30 and Joseph's role as a symbol of restored creation and of new life).
Exodus	John	
Chaps. 1–4	Chap. 4	The revelation to Moses/the woman, etc. (John 4:31–38, food and Jesus' impending death ["complete the work"]; cf. passover and unleavened bread, Exodus 12–13?).
5:1–15:21 (except chaps. 12–13)	Chap. 5	God's commanding power over creation (particularly as seen in the plagues—against the background of the countercommands of Pharaoh (cf. Exod 5:1–7:7)—and in the commanding word of Jesus), a power which raises people from slavery/lifelessness and sets them free. Some details: 1. The expectant Israel/multitude by the water at Baalzephon/Bethzatha (Exod 14:1–4,9; John 5:2–3). 2. The dividing of the water and the troubling of the Egyptian camp (Exod 14:21,25); the troubling of the water (John 5:7).

		3. The casting of the horse and rider into the sea (Exod 15:1, 21); and of someone sick into the pool (John 5:7). 4. God's glory—in contrast to human glory or military pretension (Exod 14:4, 17, 18; 15:1, 2, 6, 7, 11, 21; John 5:41, 44).
15:22–chap. 18	Chap. 6	God's providence—particularly as manifested in the giving of nourishment and teaching.
Chaps. 19–24	Chap. 7	Revealing the law. Some connections: 1. The need for careful distance and timing (Exod 19:9–25, esp. vv 11–12, 15–16, 20, 24; John 7:5–6, 8–10). 2. Teaching the law (Exod 20–23; John 7:14–24). 3. Communication with God's glory (Exod 24; John 7:37–39).
Chaps. 25–40	Chap. 8	Inner union with God (cf. Jesus' union with the Father, John 8:12–30; and Moses' union with God, Exod 32–34). The climactic arrival/departure of the divine presence (Exod 40:34–38, John 8:58–59).
Leviticus	John 9	!?
Numbers Chaps. 1–10	John Chap. 10	The divine formation of the chosen community and the consequent anointed dignity of its members. Formation and redemption (Num 1–6; John 10:1–21). Dedication and departure (Num 7–10; John 10:22–42). (As Num 1–2 is a community-

		centered variation on Genesis 1–2, John 10:7–18 is a variation on John 1:1–18. The role of the Levites in Num 1–10 has affinities with the role of humankind in Genesis 1–2 and with that of Christ in John 10).
11–19	11:1–53	At a time of life-and-death crises/crisis for the community, the Lord appears, descending into the human situation. Instead of four (?) major crises (Num 11, Num 12, Num 13–14, Num 15–19), each of which is resolved by a divine appearance (Num 11:24, 12:5, 14:10, 17:8), John gives just one.
20–36	11:54–12:50	The journey towards death and the promised land, a journey with losses and blessings. (In Numbers, cf. the death of Miriam and Aaron, intimations of the death of Moses, and other references to death, 20:1, 28; 21:6–9; 25:9; 26:10, 61, 65; 27:3, 13; also chaps. 34–36: possession of the land [34], refuge from death [35], inheritance of the land [36]).
Deuteronomy Chaps. 1–30	John Chaps. 13–17	The final discourse(s). Outline (???): Deut 1:1–4:40, John 13: God's care, human reluctance. Deut 4:41–11:32, John 14: the difficult human journey to God. Deut 12–18, John 15:1–17: God's place of true worship and communication (the temple/the vine).

Deut 19:1–26:15, John 15:18–16:4a: ?

Deut 26:16–28:58, John 16:4b–33: the difficult death-related human response to the preceding discourse (in Deut 12:1–26:15, John 15:1–16:4a).

Deut 29–30, John 17: hard-won union with God.

Chaps. 31–34   Chaps. 18–21

The final days. Outline (???):

1. Giving revelation (writing/speaking), even in face of death: Deut 31:1–13, John 18:1–27: an external revelation, given to all (cf. Brodie, *Commentary*. 1992, on John 18:1–19:16a). Deut 31:14–23, John 18:28–19:16a: an inner revelation (at the tent; within).

2. Going out in song/glory, and, in the process, building and blessing the community: Deut 31:24–32:47, John 19:16b–37: the death, the upbuilding words and the law/writing. Deut 32:48–chap. 33, John 19:38–chap. 20: the ascent and the imparting of strength and blessing. Deut 34, John 21: the evoking of a wide horizon, the suggestion (clear in John) of victory over the grave, and the emergence of a leader (Joshua/Peter). The signs.

APPENDIX D

John's Use of Part of Luke-Acts: A Tentative Outline of One Dimension

There is considerable agreement that before the development of Luke and Acts as distinct documents, the two formed a single, shorter, document. However, the precise nature and shape of that text is quite controverted. Some maintain, for instance, that in the original Luke-Acts there was no infancy narrative (Brown, 1977, 240; Fitzmyer, 1981, 310–11). Others would say that the infancy narrative was, in fact, part of the original version but that the central body of the gospel was much shorter, and that Acts finished with the climactic decision of the council of Jerusalem (at 15:35 or 15:33; see Gaston, 1970, 244–56, esp. 255–56).

Apparently it was some such version—a brief gospel followed by Acts 1:1–15:35—which was used by John. As noted earlier, in discussing John's use of Luke-Acts, John 3–4 builds systematically on aspects of Acts 5–8. And further analysis suggests that in varying ways that systematic dependence continues: John 1–8 and John 10 use the rest of Acts—but only as far as 15:35. As for the remainder of John, the dependence seems to be not on the entire third gospel but simply on parts of it. Thus the infancy narrative, with its emphasis on such elements as birth, parents, and the process of growing up (Luke 1–2), would appear to have been used to provide some of the components of John 9. And some of Luke's subsequent texts (e.g., 3:1–4:30 and 7:1–8:3) apparently contributed to John 11–12. But there are several Lukan passages which do not seem to fit the pattern. This is particularly clear in Luke 4:31–chap. 6—an extensive section, which is itself dependent on Mark and Matthew/Q. In other words, the version of Luke-Acts used by John was one which had not yet absorbed Mark and Matthew. It would also appear that this earlier version did not include much of the central section of Luke (esp. 10:21–chap. 15).

The proposal made here—as a tentative working hypothesis—is that John has made use of Luke 1–2; 3:1–6, 10–38; 4:14–30; 7:1–8:3; 9:51–10:20; 16:1–9, 19–31; 17:11–18:8; 19:1–10; 22:1–30; 22:66–chap. 24; and Acts 1:1–15:35. To some degree this proposal is based on the relationship between John and Luke. But it is also partly based on other studies, undertaken by the present writer (1979, 1983, 1984, 1986, 1986a, 1989, 1989a, 1990), concerning Luke's use of the OT. These studies indicate that in using the OT, Luke's text shows a steady pattern of dependence. And that pattern found, for instance, in much of Luke 1:1–4:30, in 7:1–8:3, and in 9:51–10:20, may be distinguished from other patterns such as Luke's dependence on Mark and on Matthew/Q.

A full exposition of this proposal would require a volume to itself. Within the context of the present study such a massive digression does not seem to be justified; from the point of view of Johannine studies, the details of the shape of the earlier form of Luke-Acts are secondary in comparison to the central fact, which can be established with relative ease—namely that John made systematic use of part of Luke-Acts. Hence for the moment the shape of the details remains unproven, a working hypothesis.

This hypothesis will help explain why—in the subsequent outline of John's apparent dependence on Luke-Acts—further claims are not made, particularly concerning John's dependence on certain passages of Luke's gospel. In seeking the origin of John 21, for instance, it might seem reasonable at first sight to suggest that there is some form of dependence on Luke's account of the fishing scene in which the sudden huge catch caused Peter to confess his sinfulness (Luke 5:1–11). But Luke 5:1–11 is embedded in the middle of that first large section (Luke 4:31–chap. 6), which is so massively dependent on Mark and Matthew/Q—a section which apparently was not part of the earlier version of Luke-Acts. Hence, despite its attractiveness, the Lukan fishing scene is not appealed to, and John 21 has to be explained through other texts (through the commissioning in Galilee: Matt 20:16–20; the call of the fishermen: Mark 1:16–20; the pictures of Peter as coming to Jesus through the water and as being commissioned: Matt 14:28–31, 16:18–

19; and so on. Because of its climactic function, chapter 21 involves an unusual synthesizing of many diverse elements and sources).

As for the resemblance between Luke 5:1–11 and John 21, that can be accounted for by saying, not that John used Luke, but that Luke used John. In other words, Luke's second edition, as well as incorporating Mark and Matthew/Q, also incorporated aspects of John. But again, as in the case of the hypothesis concerning the shape of the early edition of Luke-Acts, such a proposal, in order to be used with any reliability, would require extensive exposition. And, again, such an exposition concerning Luke-Acts does not seem appropriate in a study concerning John.

Amid so much that is unproven, the essential point remains clear: John 3–4 made systematic use of Acts 5–8. And the following tentative outline suggests that that dependence extends beyond these texts.

The outline, even if it is accurate, is not complete; it covers just one dimension of the relationship between the texts. For instance, if, as the outline suggests, the beginning of John (1:1–28) drew on the beginning of Acts (1:1–5)—Acts seems to have been among the factors which contributed to John's idea of beginning with a prologue and of empha-sizing some variation on the concept of the *logos*, "Word" (Acts 1:1, John 1:1)—that does not mean that the beginning of John used no other part of Luke-Acts or that the beginning of Acts did not contribute to other parts of John. Allowance must be made for other patterns of dependence and for some criss-crossing of elements. However, while the trail indicated by the outline may not lead to the complete story, it does appear to be significant.

Acts	John	Connection
1:1–5	1:1–28	Prologue, esp. regarding the word (cf. also Luke 4:1–4); John's bap-tism.
1:6–11	1:29–34	Jesus goes to heaven; Jesus comes as if from heaven.
1:12–26	1:35–51	The disciples and the extra disci-ple/apostle (Nathanael, Matthias).
Chap.2	2:1–11	At the right time, an outpouring of wine/Spirit.
3:1–4:31	2:12–22	The temple; the Jewish challenge; Jesus' death and resurrection.

4:32–5:16	2:23–25	Many signs and believers, yet hidden in people (in Ananias and Sapphira) there are problems.
5:17–42	3:1–21	The raising up of Jesus; witness; Gamaliel and Nicodemus.
6:1–8:1a	3:22–36	Increasing numbers and resulting discontent (murmuring/dispute). The emergence of a new order. Stephen and John bear witness to the one from heaven.
8:1b–25	4:1–42	The conversion of Samaria.
8:26–40	4:43–54	The royal official.
Chap. 9	Chap. 5	In face of the death-bearing attitude of the Jews (as seen in Saul and in the Jewish attacks on Saul), an assertion of the life-giving power of God (in raising Saul, Aeneas, Dorcas and the man at the pool).
Chap. 10	Chap. 6	Moving towards the wider gentile world (as intimated by Caesarea and Tiberias), towards accepting all the life and care that God offers to people (God's care for the Gentiles; the bread of life).
Chap. 11	Chap. 7	Despite Jewish narrowness (concerning the uncircumcised/law), the presence of a wider approach, one based not on superficiality but on Spirit. A time of stress (of attacks on Jesus, and of persecution and famine in Antioch).
Chap. 12	8:12–30	Even when there is danger of death (Peter at the hands of Herod; Jesus at the hands of the Jews) one is not alone: in darkness there is light and there is support (of prayer; of the Father).
13–14	Chap. 10	Care to bring salvation to all peo-

ple (Jews and Gentiles; sheep and "other sheep") as reflected in the missionary journey and in the figure of the good shepherd. Jewish opposition to this process (to the mission; to the good shepherd). Some details: pictures of (implied) believing (Acts 14:1, John 10:19–21); someone walking (in Solomon's porch, John 10:23; in a healing which recalls the earlier healing in Solomon's porch, Acts 14:8–10; cf. Acts 3:1–11); responding to Jewish psychological (cf. *psychas*) pressure with openness and witness (Acts 14:2–3, John 10:24–26a); work/working, blasphemy, eternal life (Acts 13:41, 45–48; John 10:26–28, 31–33a); stoning (Acts 14:5, 19); surrounding (Acts 14:20, John 10:24); division (Acts 14:4, John 10:19); humans are gods (Acts 14:11–18, John 10:33b–34); the sending, the word, the fulfillment of scripture, being God's son (?? Acts 13:26, 29, 33; John 10:35–36).

15:1–35	8:31–59	Conflict with superficial believers. The necessity of leaving aside an enslaving emphasis on externals, and of entering into the word which gives life and joy.
Luke	John	
Chaps. 1–2	Chap. 9	Birth, growing up, parents, freedom from parents, worship.
3:1–6, 14–38; 4:14–30	12:20–43	Intimations of a world-wide word which involves disturbance on

		earth and intervention from heaven. The crowd's reactions and questions. Jewish rejection of the word.
7:1–35	11:1–53	Sickness, love, death and life. Despite opposition (Luke 7:18–35, John 11:45–53) prophecy still functions and God's plan is fulfilled.
7:36–8:3, 9:51–10:20	11:54–12:19	Anointing, service, going to Jerusalem, the humble traveller (with no place to rest; on a donkey). The world mission and response. Refusal (by cities; by Pharisees).
?	12:44–50	
See 7:36–50 16:1–9, 19–31; 17:11–19	Chap. 13 Chap. 14	The feet, water, Simon's objections. Human response: the effort (working/believing) in order to have an everlasting dwelling. Concentrating on the present human reality, and not (as Lazarus, Thomas, and Philip would have it) on something visionlike or beyond the grave. The faith which leads to healing, praise, and thanksgiving (17:11–19; cf. 14:12–31).
17:20–37	15:1–16:4a	God's kingdom is within, and its coming requires great suffering.
18:1–8	16:4b–33	The human effort and faith which, despite its poverty and weakness, brings justice/joy.
19:1–10	John 17	The ascent to seeing Jesus/God leads to practical involvement in the world.
22:1–30, 66–71	18:1–27	Judas in conspiracy; Jesus knows all that will happen (22:8–13, John 18:4). Drinking the cup. Abrasive rulers. Jesus speaks openly.

23:1–25	18:28– 19:16a	Trial before Pilate.
23:26–49	19:16b–37	Crucifixion and death.
23:50–24:53	19:38–21:25	Burial (23:50–56, John 19:38–42). Resurrection (24:1–12, 20:1–10). Recognition (24:13–35, 20:10–18). Appearance and doubt (24:36–49, 20:19–27). God and blessing (24:50–53, 20:28–29). Universal mission and misunderstanding by the Jews/brothers (John 21; cf. Matt 28:10–20).

APPENDIX E

John's Main Sources:
An Approximate Summary

John	Mark	Matthew	Luke-Acts	Pentateuch (Epistles)
1	1:1–20, 2:13–17		Acts 1	Gen 1:1–4:16
2	1:21–45		Acts 2:1–4:31	Gen 4:17– chap. 11
3	2:1–12, 18–22		Acts 4:32– chap. 7	Gen 12–50
4	5:1–6:27		Acts 8	Exod 1–4
5	2:23–3:6		Acts 9	Exod 5:1–15:21
6	3:7–chap. 4, 6:30–56		Acts 10	Exod 15:22– chap. 18
7	7:1–8:10	} chaps. 5–7	Acts 11	Exod 19–24
8	13:5–23		Acts 12, 15:1–35	Exod 25–40
9	8:11–9:8		Luke 1–2	Lev?
10	?	chap. 10	Acts 13–14	Num 1–10
11	9:9–29, 14:1–9		Luke 3:1–6, 10–38; 4:14–30	Num 11–19

12	chap. 11; 13:1–4, 24–37		Luke 7:1–8:3; 9:51–10, 20	Num 20–36
13	14:10–31		cf. Luke 7:36–50	Deut 1:1–4:40
14		chap. 18	Luke 16:1–9, 19–31; 17:11–19	Deut 4:41– 11:32
15	chaps. 10, 12?	24:45–chap. 25	Luke 17:20–37	Deut 12:1– 26:15?
16			Luke 18:1–8	Deut 26:16– 26:68
17	14:32–42		Luke 19:1–10	Deut 29–30 (Ephesians)
18				Deut 31:1–23
19	14:43–chap. 16	(26:47–chap. 28)	Luke 22:1–30	Deut 31:24– 32:47
20			Luke 22:30– chap. 24	Deut 32:48– chap. 33
21				Deut 34

Bibliography

AB	Anchor Bible.
ANRW	*Aufstieg und Niedergand der Römischen Welt.*
ASNU	Acta seminarii neotestamentici upsaliensis.
BETL	Bibliotheca ephemeridum theologicarum lovaniensium.
Bib	*Biblica.*
BZ	*Biblische Zeitschrift.*
CBQ	*Catholic Biblical Quarterly.*
DBSup	*Dictionnaire de la Bible, Supplement.*
De Jonge	M. de Jonge, ed. *L'évangile de Jean: Sources. rédaction, théologie.* BETL 44. Leuven: Leuven University, 1977.
ETL	*Ephemerides theologicae lovaniensis.*
ExpTim	*Expository Times.*
HUCA	*Hebrew Union College Annual.*
Int	*Interpretation.*
JB	Jerusalem Bible.
JBL	*Journal of Biblical Literature.*
JSNT	*Journal for the Study of the New Testament.*
JTS	*Journal of Theological Studies.*
KJV	King James Version.
LumVie	*Lumière et Vie.*
NAB	New American Bible.
NCeB	New Century Bible Commentary.
NEB	New English Bible.
NJBC	*New Jerome Biblical Commentary.* Ed. by R. E. Brown *et al.* Englewood Cliffs, N.J.: Prentice Hall, 1990.
NovT	*Novum Testamentum.*
NovTSup	*Novum Testamentum, Supplements.*
NTS	*New Testament Studies.*

ÖTKNT   Ökumenischer Taschenbuchkommentar zum Neuen
         Testament.
RA   *Religions in Antiquity. Essays in Memory of E. R.*
         Goodenough. Ed. by J. Neusner. Numen Suppl. 14;
         Leiden: Brill, 1968.
RB   *Revue Biblique.*
RevThom *Revue Thomiste.*
RSV   Revised Standard Version.
SBL   Society of Biblical Literature.
SBLDS   SBL Dissertation Series.
ScEs   *Science et esprit.*
SE   *Studia Evangelica.*
SNTSMS   Society for New Testament Studies Monograph Series.
SUNT   Studien zur Umwelt des Neuen Testaments.
TS   *Theological Studies.*
TZ   *Theologische Zeitschrift.*
UBSGNT   United Bible Societies *Greek New Testament.*
VT   *Vetus testamentum.*
WMANT   Wissenschaftliche Monographien zum Alten und Neuen
         Testament.
ZAW   *Zeitschrift für die alttestamentliche Wissenschaft.*
ZNW   *Zeitschrift fur die neutestamentliche Wissenschaft.*

Commentaries, Cited by Author Only

Barrett, C. K. The Gospel According to St. John. 2d ed. Philadelphia: Westminster, 1978. (1st ed., 1955)

Beasley-Murray, G. R. *John.* Word Biblical Commentary 36. Waco, Tex: Word Books, 1987.

Becker, J. *Das Evangelium nach Johannes.* ÖTKNT 4. 2 vols. Würzburg: Echter, 1979, 1981.

Brown, R. E. *The Gospel According to John.* AB. 2 vols. Garden City, N.Y.: Doubleday, 1966–71.

Bultmann, R. *The Gospel of John. A Commentary.* Philadelphia: Westminster, 1971. (German ed., 1941.)

Hoskyns, E. C. *The Fourth Gospel.* Ed. F. N. Davey. 2d ed. London: Faber & Faber, 1947.

Lindars, B. *The Gospel of John.* NCeB. Grand Rapids, Mich.: Eerdmans, 1972.

Schnackenburg, R. *The Gospel According to St. John.* 3 vols. New York: Crossroad, 1968–82. (German ed., 1965–75.)

Bibliographies

Malatesta, E. 1967. *St. John's Gospel 1920–1965. A Cumulative and Classified Bibliography of Books and Periodical Literature on the Fourth Gospel.* Rome: Pontifical Biblical Institute.

Van Belle, G. 1988. *Johannine Bibliography 1966–1985. A Cumulative Bibliography on the Fourth Gospel.* Leuven: Leuven University / Peeters.

Wagner, G. 1987. *An Exegetical Bibliography of the New Testament. John and 1, 2, 3 John.* Macon, Ga.: Mercer University.

Other Works

Alter, R. 1981. *The Art of Biblical Narrative.* New York: Basic Books.

———. 1985. *The Art of Biblical Poetry.* New York: Basic Books.

Attridge, H. W. 1976. *The Interpretation of Biblical History in the Antiquitates Judaicae of Flavius Josephus.* HDR 7. Missoula, Mont.: Scholars.

———. 1985. "Gnosticism." *Harpers Bible Dictionary.* (ed. P. J. Achtemeier; San Francisco: Harper & Row, 1985) 349–50.

———. 1989. "John and Some Gnostics." Paper given at Catholic Biblical Association convention, Syracuse, N.Y., August 17, 1989.

Auerbach, E. 1953. *Mimesis. The Representation of Reality in Western Literature.* Princeton: Princeton University.

Aune, D. 1987. *The New Testament in Its Literary Environment.* Philadelphia: Westminster.

———. 1988. Ed. *Greco-Roman Literature and the New Testament. Selected Forms and Genres.* SBLSBS 21. Atlanta, Ga.: Scholars.

Baldensperger, W. 1898. *Der Prolog des vierten Evangeliums, sein polemisch-apologetischer Zweck.* Freiburg i. Breisgau.

Barrett, C. K. 1972. "The Dialectical Theology of St. John." In: *New Testament Essays.* Ed. C. K. Barrett. London: SPCK, 49–69.

———. 1974. "John and the Synoptic Gospels." *ExpTim* 85:228–33.

———. 1975. *The Gospel of John and Judaism.* Philadelphia: Fortress.

Baumgartner, W. 1950. "Der heutige Stand der Mandäerfrage". *TZ* 6:401–10.

Becker, U. 1963. *Jesus und die Ehebrecherin. Untersuchungen zur Text- und Überlieferungsgeschichte von Joh 7:53–8:11.* BZNW 28. Berlin: Töpelmann.

Bloch, R. 1957. "Midrash." DBSup V: 1263–81.

Boismard, M. E. 1988. *Moïse ou Jésus. Essai de Christolgie Johannique.* BETL 84. Leuven: Leuven University / Peeters.

Boismard, M.-E. and Lamouille A. 1977. *L'Evangile de Jean. Synopse des quatre évangiles.* Vol. 3 Paris: du Cerf.

Boomershine, T. E. 1985. Review of Kelber, 1983. *JBL* 104:535–40.

Bowra, C. M. 1945. *From Virgil to Milton*. New York and London: Macmillan.

Braun, F. M. 1955. "Hermétisme et Johannisme." *RevThom* 55:22–42, 259–99.

Brodie, T. L. 1979. "A New Temple and a New Law. The Unity and Chronicler-based Nature of Luke 1:1–4:22a." *JSNT* 5:21–45.

———. 1981. "Jesus as the New Elisha: Cracking the Code [John 9]." *ExpTim* 93:39–42.

———. 1983. "The Accusing and Stoning of Naboth (1 Kgs. 21:8–13) as One Component of the Stephen Text (Acts 6:9–14; 7:58a)." *CBQ* 45:417–32.

———. 1983a. "Luke 7,36–50 as an Internalization of 2 Kings 4,1–37: A Study in Luke's Use of Rhetorical Imitation." *Bib* 64:457–85.

———. 1984. "Greco-Roman Imitation of Texts as a Partial Guide to Luke's Use of Sources." In *Luke-Acts. New Perspectives from the Society of Biblical Literature*. Ed. C. H. Talbert. New York: Crossroad.

———. 1984a. Review of Kelber, 1983. *CBQ* 46:574–75.

———. 1986. "Towards Unravelling Luke's Use of the Old Testament: Luke 7.11–17 as an *Imitatio* of 1 Kings 17.17–24." *NTS* 32:247–67.

———. 1986a. "Towards Unravelling the Rhetorical Imitation of Sources in Acts: 2 Kgs 5 as One Component of Acts 8,9–40." *Bib* 67:1986.

———. 1989. "The Departure for Jerusalem (Luke 9,51–56) as a Rhetorical Imitation of Elijah's Departure for the Jordan (2 Kgs 1,1–2,6)" *Bib* 70:96–109.

———. 1989a. "Luke 9:57–62: A Systematic Adaptation of the Divine Challenge to Elijah (1 Kings 19)." *SBL Seminar Papers*. Atlanta, Ga.: Scholars, 237–45.

———. 1990. "Luke-Acts as an Imitation and Emulation of the Elijah-Elisha Narrative." In *New Views on Luke and Acts*. Ed. E. Richard. Collegeville, Minn.: Liturgical, and Wilmington, DE: Glazier, 78–85.

———. 1992. *The Gospel According to John. A Literary and Theological Commentary*. New York and Oxford: Oxford University.

Brown, R. E. 1961. "Incidents that are Units in the Synoptic Gospels but Dispersed in St. John." *CBQ* 23:143–60.

———. 1977. *The Birth of the Messiah. A Commentary on the Infancy Narratives in Matthew and Luke*. Garden City, N.Y.: Doubleday.

———. 1978. Review of *L'Evangile de Jean*. M.-E. Boismard and A. Lamouille.) *CBQ* 40:624–28.

———. 1979. *The Community of the Beloved Disciple*. New York: Paulist.

———. 1982. *The Epistles of John*. AB. Garden City, N.Y.: Doubleday.

Buchanan, G. 1968. "The Samaritan Origin of the Gospel of John." *RA* 149–75.

Bultmann, R. 1955. *Theology of the New Testament*. Vol. 2. London: SCM.

————. 1958. *Der Geschichte der synoptischen Tradition*. Göttingen: Vandenhoeck & Ruprecht. 3d ed.

————. 1963. *The History of the Synoptic Tradition*. New York: Harper & Row, 1963. (English translator of Bultmann, 1958.)

Burkitt, F. C. 1928. "The Mandaeans." *JTS* 29:225–37.

Caird, G. B. 1976. "The Study of the Gospels: II. Form Criticism." *ExpTim* 87:137–41.

Childs, B. S. 1985. *The New Testament as Canon*. Philadelphia: Fortress.

Conington, J. 1963. *The Works of Virgil*. Vol. 2. Hildesheim: Georg Olms.

Costa, C. N. D. 1973. *Seneca, Medea*. Oxford: Clarendon.

Cullmann, O. 1930. *Le problème littéraire et historique du roman pseudoclémentin*. Paris: F. Alcan.

————. 1976. *The Johannine Circle*. Philadelphia: Westminster.

Culpepper, R. A. 1975. *The Johannine School: An Evaluation of the Johannine-School Hypothesis Based on an Investigation of the Nature of Ancient Schools*. SBLDS 26. Missoula, Mont.: Scholars.

De Jonge, M. (ed.) 1977. *L'Evangile de Jean. Sources, rédaction, théologie*. BETL XLIV. Louvain: Leuven University; and Gembloux: J. Duculot.

Dodd, C. H. 1953. *The Interpretation of the Fourth Gospel*. Cambridge: Cambridge University.

————. 1963. *Historical Tradition in the Fourth Gospel*. Cambridge: Cambridge University.

Dubois, J.-D. 1980. "La postérité du quatrième évangile au deuxième siècle." *LumVie* 29(149).31–50.

Dunn, J. D. G. 1986, Review of Kelber, 1983. *Int* 40:72–75.

Fischer, G. 1975. *Die himmlischen Wohnungen. Untersuchungen zu Joh 14, 2f*. Bern: Lang.

Fishbane, M. 1985. *Biblical Interpretation in Ancient Israel*. New York and Oxford: Oxford University.

————. 1986. "Inner Biblical Exegesis: Types and Strategies of Interpretation in Ancient Israel." In *Midrash and Literature* (Ed. G. H. Hartman and S. Budick.) New Haven and London: Yale University, 19–37.

Fiske, G. C. 1920. *Lucilius and Horace: A Study in the Classical Theory of Imitation*. Madison, WI: University of Wisconsin. (Reprint ed. Westport, Conn.: Greenwood.)

Fitzmyer, J. A. 1962. "Memory and Manuscript: The Origins and Transmission of the Gospel Tradition." *TS* 23:442–57.

————. 1981. *The Gospel According to Luke I–IX*. AB 28. Garden City, N.Y.: Doubleday.

Fortna, R. T. 1970. *The Gospel of Signs: A Reconstruction of the Narrative Source Underlying the Fourth Gospel*. SNTSMS 11. Cambridge: Cambridge University.

182   *Bibliography*

———. 1988. *The Fourth Gospel and Its Predecessor. From Narrative Source to Present Gospel.* Philadelphia: Fortress.

Freed, E. D. 1970. "Did John Write His Gospel Partly to Win Samaritan Converts?" *NovT* 12:241–56.

Fujita, N. S. 1986. *A Crack in the Jar. What Ancient Jewish Documents Tell Us About the New Testament.* New York and Mahwah, N.J.: Paulist.

Gardner-Smith, P. 1938. *Saint John and the Synoptic Gospels.* Cambridge: Cambridge University.

Gaston, L. 1970. *No Stone on Another. Studies in the Significance of the Fall of Jerusalem in the Synoptic Gospels.* Leiden: Brill.

Gerhardsson, B. 1961. *Memory and Manuscript: Oral Tradition and Written Transmission in Rabbinic Judaism and Early Christianity.* ASNU 22. Lund: Gleerup.

———. 1964. *Tradition and Transmission in Early Christianity.* Lund: Gleerup.

———. 1979. *The Origins of the Gospel Tradition.* Philadelphia: Fortress.

Greene, T. M. 1963. *The Descent from Heaven. A Study in epic Continuity.* New Haven/London: Yale University.

Greene, T. M. 1963. *The Descent from Heaven. A Study in Epic Continuity.* New Haven and London: Yale University.

Gunkel, H. 1901. *Genesis, überstezt und erklärt.* Göttingen: Vandenhoeck & Ruprecht.

Harrigan, U. 1984. "*Ulysses* as Missal: Another Structure in James Joyce's *Ulysses.*" *Christianity and Literature* 33:35–50.

Harrington, D. J. 1986. "Palestinian Adaptations of Biblical Narratives and Prophecies. I. The Bible Rewritten (Narratives)." In *Early Judaism and Its Modern Interpreters.* (Ed. R. A. Kraft and G. W. E. Nickelsburg.) Atlanta, Ga.: Scholars, 239–47.

Hengel, M. 1974. *Judaism and Hellenism.* Philadelphia: Fortress.

———. 1989. *The Johannine Question.* London: SCM, and Philadelphia: Trinity Press International.

Higginbotham, J. 1969. Ed. *Greek and Latin Literature.* London: Methuen.

Holladay, C. R. 1983, 1989. *Fragments from Hellenistic Jewish Authors.* 2 vols. Atlanta, Ga.: Scholars.

Hurtado, L. W. 1983. *Mark. A Good News Commentary.* San Francisco: Harper & Row.

Kealy, S. P. 1982. *Mark's Gospel. A History of Its Interpretation.* New York: Paulist.

Kelber, W. H. 1974. *The Kingdom in Mark. A New Place and a New Time.* Philadelphia: Fortress.

———. 1983. *The Oral and Written Gospel.* Philadelphia: Fortress.

Knauer, G. N. 1979. *Die Aeneis und Homer.* Hypomnemata 7. Göttingen: Vandenhoeck & Ruprecht.

Kügler, J. 1984. "Das Johannesevangelium und seine Gemeinde—kein Thema für Science Fiction." *Biblische Notizen* 23:48–62.

Kurz, W. 1980. "Hellenistic Rhetoric in the Christological Proof of Luke-Acts." *CBQ* 42: 171–95.

Kysar, R. 1985. "The Fourth Gospel. A Report on Recent Research." *ANRW* 2(25.3)2391–480.

Lee, G. 1981. "Imitation and the Poetry of Virgil." *Greece and Rome* 28:10–22.

Lesky, A. 1966. *A History of Greek Literature.* 2d ed. New York: Crowell.

MacRae, G. W. 1970. "The Fourth Gospel and Religionsgeschichte." *CBQ* 32:17–24.

Malherbe, A. J. 1989. *Paul and the Popular Philosophers.* Philadelphia: Fortress.

Mann, C. S. 1986. *Mark. A New Translation with Introduction and Commentary.* AB. Garden City, New York: Doubleday.

Martin, F. 1988. *Narrative Parallels to the New Testament.* Atlanta, Ga.: Scholars.

Martyn, J. L. 1968, 1979. *History and Theology in the Fourth Gospel.* 2d ed. Nashville, Tenn.: Abingdon. (First ed., 1968).

————. 1978. *The Gospel of John in Christian History.* New York, Ramsey, N.J., and Toronto: Paulist.

Mattill, A. J. 1977. "Johannine Communities Behind the Fourth Gospel: Georg Richter's Analysis." *TS* 38:294–315.

Maynard, A. 1985. "Ti emoi kai soi." *NTS* 31:582–86.

Meeks, W. 1972. "The Man from Heaven in Johannine Sectarianism." *JBL* 91:44–72.

Moran, W. L. 1969. "Deuteronomy." In *A New Catholic Commentary on Holy Scripture.* London: Nelson, 256–76.

Neirynck, F. 1975. "The 'Other Disciple' in Jn 18,15–16." *ETL* 51: 113–41.

————. 1977. "John and the Synoptics." In de Jonge, 1977, 73–106.

————. 1983. "De Semeia-Bron in het Vierde Evangelie: Kritiek van een Hypothese." *Academiae Analecta*, Klasse der Lettern 45:1–28.

————. 1984a. "John and the Synoptics: The Empty Tomb Stories." *NTS* 30:161–87.

————. 1984b. "John 4,46–54: Signs Source and/or Synoptic Gospels." *ETL* 60:367–75.

Neyrey, J. 1988. *An Ideology of Revolt. John's Christology in Social Science Perspective.* Philadelphia: Fortress.

Nicol, W. 1972. *The Sēmeia in the Fourth Gospel. Tradition and Redaction.* Leiden: Brill.

O'Leary, P. 1991. "The Church: Leaking at the Edges?" Paper given at Dominican Studium, Tallaght, Dublin, Dec. 3, 1991.

Ong, W. J. 1971. *Rhetoric, Romance and Technology.* Ithaca, N.Y., and London: Cornell University.

———. 1977. *Interfaces of the Word. Studies in the Evolution of Consciousness and Culture.* Ithaca, N.Y.: Cornell University.

Onuki, T. 1984. *Gemeinde und Welt im Johannesevangelium: Ein Beitrag zur Frage nach der theologischen und pragmatischen Funktion des johanneischen "Dualismus."* WMANT 56. Neukirchen-Vluyn: Neukirchener.

Pagels, E. 1989. *The Johannine Gospel in Gnostic Exegesis. Heracleon's Commentary on John.* Atlanta, Ga.: Scholars.

Pearce, K. 1985. "The Lucan Origins of the Raising of Lazarus." *ExpTim* 96:359–61.

Plümacher, E. 1972. *Lukas als hellenistischer Schriftsteller.* SUNT 9. Göttingen: Vandenhoeck & Ruprecht.

Porton, G. 1979. "Midrash: Palestinian Jews and the Hebrew Bible in the Greco-Roman Period. *ANRW* 19(2):103–8.

———. 1985. *Understanding Rabbinic Midrash.* Hoboken, N.J.: KTAV.

Rehm, B. Ed. 1965. *Die Pseudoklementinen, II, Rekognitionen.* Berlin: Academie.

Reim, G. 1988. "Zur Lokalisierung der johanneischen Gemeinde." *BZ* 32: 72–86.

Rensberger, D. 1988. *Johannine Faith and Liberating Community.* Philadelphia: Westminster.

Richter, G. 1975. "Präsentische und futurische Eschatologie im 4. Evangelium." In *Gegenwart und Kommendes Reich* (A. Vögtle Schulergabe; ed. P. Fiedler and D. Zeller.) Stuttgart: Katholisches Bibelwerk, 117–52.

Sabbe, M. 1977. "The Arrest of Jesus in Jn 18,1–11 and its Relation to the Synoptic Gospels: A Critical Evaluation of A. Dauer's Hypothesis." In de Jonge, 1977, 203–34.

Schnackenburg, R. 1977. "Johanneische Forschung seit 1955." In De Jonge, 1977, 19–44.

Schottroff, L. 1970. *Der Glaubende und die feindliche Welt: Beobachtungen zum gnostischen Dualismus und seiner Bedeutung für Paulus und das Johannesevangelium.* WMANT. Neukirchen: Neukirchener.

Selong, G. 1971. *The Cleansing of the Temple in Jn 2, 13–22, with a Reconsideration of the Dependence of the Fourth Gospel upon the Synoptics.* Dissertation, Leuven. Abstracted in *ETL* 48(1972):212–13.

Smith, D. M. 1982. "John and the Synoptics." *Bib* 63:102–13.

———. 1984. *Johannine Christianity. Essays on the Setting, Sources and Theology.* Columbia, S.C.: University of South Carolina.

Steiner, G. 1975. *After Babel: Aspects of Language and Translation.* New York and London: Oxford University.

Stock, A. 1982. *Call to Discipleship. A Literary Study of Mark's Gospel.* Wilmington, Del.: Glazier.

Van Belle, G. 1975. *De Semeia-Bron in het Vierde Evangelie: Ontstaan en groe; van een hypothese.* Leuven: Leuven University.

Vermes, G. 1961. *Scripture and Tradition in Judaism.* Leiden: Brill.

von Wahlde, U. C. 1989. *The Earliest Version of John's Gospel. Recovering the Gospel of Signs.* Wilmington, Del.: Glazier.

Warner, S. M. 1979. "Primitive Saga Men." *VT* 29:325–35.

Wengst, K. 1983. *Bedrängte Gemeinde und verherrlichter Christus. Der historische Ort des Johannesevangeliums als Schlüssel zu seiner Interpretation.* 2d ed. Biblisch-theologische Studien 5. Neukirchen-Vluyn: Neukirchener. (First ed., 1981.)

White, H. O. 1935. *Plagiarism and Imitation During the English Renaissance.* Cambridge: Harvard University.

Index to Modern Authors

Subject Index